S0-BMA-681

Library Instruction in the Elementary School

by

Melvyn K. Bowers

The Scarecrow Press, Inc.
Metuchen, N.J. 1971

ISBN 0-8108-0391-7

Library of Congress Catalog Card Number 72-155283

Photo credits: Mr. George Jagger
Sound and Service Co.
Glenhaven, California

Dedicated to my wife who, now that this is finished, may speak to me again, and to any librarian or teacher who will publish his own instructional content and methods, and so share his knowledge and experience with the rest of us who are constantly seeking improvements in our own programs.

CONTENTS

INTRODUCTION

When Gutenberg invented the printing press and opened the gates to a tremendous flood of printed material, it became imperative that man perfect a library system which would not only permit storage of the world's knowledge, but would expedite its easy retrieval and circulation. In recent years the task has been further compounded by the increase in audio-visual and related materials that have become a part of most libraries' collections. Despite the problems, many libraries have met the challenge.

Today's school library is not a dusty tomb of silence, but a beehive of varied, quiet, activity. Gone is the Victorian "keeper of the books," replaced by a dynamic, skilled professional with a keen knowledge of the age groups with which he works.

The expanding scope and services, and the increasing need for school libraries at all levels have created many problems beyond the storage and retrieval of information. One of these, the role of the school library as an instructional center in the elementary schools, is discussed by Mr. Bowers in this book. Here he presents materials and methods that, for him, have been successful in not only developing among students a healthy attitude toward libraries and library materials, but also in imparting the information necessary to develop skills in using a library and its resources.

Joseph G. Hibbs

Chapter 1

The School Library and Its Instructional Program: Definition, Need, Limitations

It is difficult, if not impossible, to present a definition of a library in a short simple statement, because a library is a marriage of planned space and climate, materials, services, instruction and personnel which operate as an integral part of the entire school environment.

A school library is space. It is space planned to properly store, retrieve and circulate the many materials which are the necessary library tools of an effective educational program. Space is needed for an entire class, for a small group, or for a single student to browse, read or work by himself. Space is necessary to help create the friendly, helpful, pleasant climate that will both attract patrons to the facility and be conducive to a healthy study and browsing environment.

A school library is material. Not only books, pamphlets, clippings and other printed material are found in the library, but also pictures, films, records, maps, tapes, realia, and all the other tools necessary to satisfy the educational needs and personal interests of today's children and their teachers. A library must lead in the selection of the materials, and then organize, catalog, shelve, file, display and advertise these items in such a manner that patrons are aware of them, and so that they may be easily retrieved, circulated and returned. The administrative methods used to accomplish this task must be those recognized by the profession as being good library practice. This is necessary to maintain a high degree of uniformity between various school libraries, so that children, moving from one system to another, or advancing to higher levels of education, will experience no great difficulty in using the facilities.

A school library is service. For itself alone, there is no reason for a library to exist. Its value lies in the unique services it provides, and its materials, facilities and personnel can be justified only through the contributions of these services to the educational program of the school. Besides the storage and circulation of its material, the library is able to perform other services which are demanded by the school system. Though these will vary to some extent between schools since demands may be somewhat different, there are services that are common to all libraries:

1. Perhaps the most important service is reading guidance. The professional librarian uses his knowledge of materials, of the individual child's interests and abilities, of the school curriculum, and of individual teacher's methods and philosophies to help children in the selection of materials for their work, special interests, leisure reading and, occasionally, to help solve a personal problem.

2. The library also provides resource services for the children and faculty. It provides needed material of all types from its own collection or from outside sources, when necessary, to any individual or area in the school. In many systems, the librarian also provides and assists with necessary hardware to provide sound, lighting, photography

or other special materials when and where it is needed. The library assists the teachers in the selection and preparation of their own materials, either for classroom work or for their own personal interests or professional growth, and assists with in-service training programs and curriculum materials and their administration, and in plant and equipment development and improvement. Contributions are made through the library publicity program that assist in maintaining the school in a good public image, and the specialized knowledge of the librarian is utilized in the formulation of policies and in establishing procedures.

There are many other services that can be performed by the experienced librarian who makes himself aware of the problems of the school. These may range from assisting a teacher with the construction of a bulletin board to locating a pen pal for a little girl. The complete range of services that a library can provide is dependent upon the need of the particular school and the adequacy of library staffing.

The school library is an instructional center. While a library does have some subject matter of its own, such as the use of the card catalog, its teaching responsibilities should not be limited to these, for there are many other areas from the school curriculum that can probably be taught more efficiently in the atmosphere of the library than in the classroom. Such areas as reference skills, techniques of reporting and literature are examples. The materials needed for the work are readily available, a trained person is available either to offer the instruction or to assist the teacher with the work, and often the change from classroom to the library is relaxing and the work less arduous, especially for the child who may have little interest in formal school work.

Because the work of the library as an instructional center involves subject matter required or desirable in all other areas of the school, it is vitally necessary for the librarian, staff and administrator to work together in developing the teaching content for the library's share in the instructional program of the school, and the actual instruction must involve both the teacher and the librarian in order to attain maximum effectiveness.

The School library is personnel. Personnel includes the classified help but the most important personnel factor is the professional librarian who is responsible for the administration and success of the library program. He must be thoroughly trained in the fields of library science and curriculum materials, besides possessing a history of successful classroom teaching experience. He is able to use this training and experience to implement all the other areas of the library. Where a library personnel is inadequate, either in training or experience, or in the number of trained persons, the library program cannot operate at a high level of efficiency and make the contributions to the school program which justify its existance.

The professional librarian provides some services as a specialized resource person which are not an actual part of the library program. He may be called upon to present his part of the school program to the public, to civic groups or professional organizations. He will be called upon to assist the administration and governing board in reaching decisions which involve his area or related areas, and will represent the school at meetings and other activities at all professional levels. Through suggestions and other means, he brings to the attention of the staff current articles and materials which help keep them informed, and he assists with professional recruitment.

The professional librarian should be many things to a school, but first and above all he is a teacher.

Need

Perhaps the simplest way to express the need for libraries is to relate the materials and services provided by the library to the body of knowledge a modern day student needs to master, and the teaching tools and methods that are needed by his teachers to accomplish the task.

The boy or girl of Ancient Egypt had a relatively small body of knowledge to master as compared to the child of today, and the teacher required tools and materials that by today's standards would be simple and few. Since that early time, each succeeding generation has pushed the frontiers of knowledge further and further, to the point where the student of today is concerning himself with things which were not even in existence when his parents were in school.

To meet the ever-increasing demands of this expanding body of knowledge, educators have found it necessary not only to expand the school curriculum and develop new methods of teaching, but also to increase greatly the quantity and complexity of the tools and materials required in the classrooms.

If each classroom were to be equipped with all the materials and tools needed to meet educational demands, each teacher would need, in addition to his present training, to be carefully trained in the selection, care and maintenance of this array of material, and would somehow have to find the time in an already busy day to catalog, store and utilize them. The administrator would be confronted with the necessity of redesigning classrooms to contain all of this material, and the high cost-use ratio and duplication of material would make education much more expensive even than it is today.

The answer lies, of course, in the library. Here the trained librarian accepts the leadership and responsibility for selection, care, and maintenance. Unnecessary duplication is avoided, cost-use ratios are kept at an acceptable level, and the school is able to provide a far broader range of services than could possibly be offered otherwise.

A school system without library services, or with inadequate facilities, can still present an educational program to the children in its community, but it can hardly achieve excellence on a high level of accomplishment.

Limitations

Of the several aspects of the library's program in the school, the one of concern here is teaching the use of the library and its materials.

Most school libraries have some form of written plan and grade placement for the various topics taught in the library. When twenty-two of these were compared, the only differences of any importance were in the amount of material covered, and in the teaching of some of the reference tools. Those schools which had adequate staffing apparently had more time to devote to instructional duties, and were able to offer more expanded programs than the others. Some schools offered a more complete reference service and found it necessary to teach the use of more tools.

The various plans proved to be so similar in construction that it was not difficult to prepare a list of suggested topics that appeared to be common to most elementary school libraries. Topics that appeared only occasionally in the plans are given in the final chapter as supplementary, along with suggested activities related to the instructional program.

Since all of the topics mentioned in the outline have been taught at the East Lake School in Clearlake Oaks, California, the suggested methods are those found to have proven successful in this system. Occasional mention is made of techniques that failed. This does not mean that such techniques may have no value, but that the experienced librarian should give them careful consideration before attempting similar methods, and the inexperienced person would probably be wise to avoid them.

It must be emphasized that any plan of instruction, such as presented here, should not be considered as a final solution to the problems faced in the instructional program of the library. Each school must tailor its own plan to meet its own particular needs. The greatest value of plans such as this one lies in its use as a guide in the development of a school's instructional program, as a comparison for evaluation of a program already in existence, and in the suggested techniques for teaching the various topics.

Chapter 2

Administration of the Instructional Program

Scheduling

Of all the administrative problems in the library, scheduling probably presents the greatest difficulty since it is one of the few activities that involves all members of the teaching staff and influences the entire school curriculum.

It is impractical to consider the instructional period without discussing the entire library schedule, for these periods must interlock with the other activities of the library in order to preserve the unity which is necessary to avoid confusion and conflict. A good library schedule should provide for the following:

1. The selection, processing, ordering and other administrative duties the librarian must perform at a time when he is able to work with a minimum of interruptions;

2. The school staff must have time to use the library facilities and have the librarian's assistance if they desire;

3. Each class should have reserved time in the library to assure the teacher sufficient space for his class, and the assistance of the librarian at this time;

4. Time is required for training clerks, for work with student librarians, the library club, meeting with school newspaper reporters and related activities;

5. "Open" periods are needed for use by anyone who wishes to use the facilities of the library or have the

assistance of the library staff;

6. Each class must have time for its instructional period in the library.

The problem of scheduling is further compounded by the fact that the library does not engage in each of these activities every day. Thus it is necessary to develop a schedule covering at least a week, and some librarians find it practical to develop a schedule covering an even longer span of time.

At Clearlake Oaks the library instructional program in the intermediate and upper grade levels is considered as a regular part of the reading program and one period of the reading class is given each week to the library. The day is selected by the classroom teacher and, generally, all the classes in any given grade will have their instructional period scheduled at the same time.

Once the instructional periods have been established, each teacher selects a period during the week for reservation. This does not indicate that the library is closed to everyone during these periods, but at these scheduled times the teacher is assured sufficient space for his class and the availability of the librarian. Other teachers may send groups or individuals to the library during these reserved periods, but with the understanding that if the teacher who holds the reservation is using the facilities, the librarian may not have a great deal of time to give individualized help to other students.

The primary and upper grades have staggered lunch hours, making it possible for the primary grades to have their library time scheduled during the period following their lunch hour. Though this method of scheduling places some limits on the choice of time for the primary teachers, the quiet activity of the library following the lunch hour appears to have some benefits for the children. These teachers have full use of the open blocks of time on the same basis as the other grades.

The one exception in this schedule is the Kindergarten. This department operates on a morning and afternoon session. The morning session requires its own block to time, and the teacher selects one-half of a regular open period for her use. The afternoon session is scheduled the same as the other primary grades.

The "open" periods where no activity is scheduled are used by individuals, groups or classes for any activity which requires the use of the facilities or the assistance of the library staff or its services. Occasionally these periods are used by the librarian for individualized help to students who may not be performing at a satisfactory level in the instructional program, or to recent arrivals to the system who have no library background. The library is never used as a general study hall. To fill the space and time with people doing work which does not require the facilities or services of the staff seriously limits the availability of the library and librarian to those who need the materials and services, and so defeats the purpose of the library.

The library schedule at Clearlake Oaks is presented on page 19 as an illustration of one approach to scheduling.

Other schools will have different scheduling problems, and will meet them in different ways. No hard and fast rules can be established which will solve any problem in all situations. No matter how the problems are resolved, no library can operate at maximum benefit to the school system unless it has the capabilities in space, time and personnel to run a well organized, full time schedule.

	Monday	Tuesday	Wednesday	Thursday	Friday
8:00- 9:00	--------	Librarian's	administrative	duties	-------------
9:00-10:00	---- and	Staff use Kindergarten	4th grade Reserved		6th grade Instruction
10:00-11:00	4th grade Instruction			Primary Reserved	
11:00-12:00					5th grade Instruction
12:00-12:30	------------	Lunch	period	------------	------------
12:30- 1:00	2nd grade Instruction	Kindergarten	3rd grade Instruction	Primary Reserved	1st grade Instruction
1:00- 2:00	5th grade Reserved				8th grade Instruction
2:00- 3:00	7th grade Reserved	8th grade Reserved	6th grade Reserved		7th grade Instruction
3:00- 3:40		Student Librarians Library Club			A-V Repair
3:40- 4:00	-----------	Administrative duties,	staff use	----------	----------

Scheduling within the instructional period will vary according to the material being presented, the particular situation that happens to face the librarian at any moment, and the methods of teaching being used. Each period must include time for browsing, selection, charging and cleaning up, in addition to the planned group activity. The following daily period schedule is typical of most library instructional periods at Clearlake Oaks.

10-15 minutes of instruction, sharing, story telling or other organized activity.

20-25 minutes of browsing, selection, renewing and charging materials.

5 minutes to replace magazines, chairs, and otherwise make the library ready for the next period.

When there are large classes in the library more time may be needed for the cleaning up process, but this time can be kept to a minimum by maintaining an orderly procedure.

Throughout this book, the material is presented with the assumption that the librarian will present his work to a single group or grade level at each of the instructional periods. An alternative is the use of the rotation system. Here the various activities are assigned to stations within the library, and the children rotate from station to station during the period.

This latter plan of operation works well where the group is very large, or in those systems which are multigraded or are operating on an ungraded and individualized plan. Though the plan is dependent upon sufficient space to separate the stations adequately, and upon sufficient personnel to man the stations, it seems to work quite well. Its chief failing lies in the fact that one or another station usually has to be manned by a classroom teacher. While most of them are willing and capable, there is the occasional teacher who wants to send his class to the library and then disappear into the teacher's lounge, or who declares that the library is the realm of the librarian and that he wants to have nothing to do with it. In such a situation the librarian may find it impossible to man the stations, and must seek other methods for handling the group.

Rules of the Instructional Period

Any orderly society has rules to govern its actions, and the library is no exception. Though there are general rules for the use of the library, a few others may be needed specifically for the instructional period. Those rules which affect the operation of the school or involve the teaching staff or the status of the library should be included in the over-all school policies. Once again, using Clearlake Oaks as an example, a set of rules is illustrated:

> From school policy:
>
> 1. The library is a regularly scheduled period, and the students must be in attendance unless excused by the librarian.
>
> 2. Teachers will accompany their classes to the library and take part in the instructional program.
>
> From the Children's Handbook
>
> 1. The rule "Quiet" will be observed at all times in the library. When discussion is necessary, please schedule a conference room.
>
> 2. Everyone will be required to find something to read or examine during the browsing portion of the period, even if he is not going to charge any material at this time.
>
> 3. Materials will be renewed or charged only during the browsing part of the period. This will

prevent interruptions and give the student librarians time to do their work.

4. If you need to be excused from the period, or part of it, please see the librarian before class begins.

5. Anytime you have a question or need help, ask the librarian or your teacher. This way you learn.

Discipline

The librarian generally enjoys a favored position in discipline matters because he usually does not have the children for as long during the day as the classroom teacher does. His brief instructional program will usually be well within the attention span of the class members and most children will find something of interest among the varied materials housed in the library. And, since he has had many of the children from Kindergarten, he has had the opportunity to develop into habit the few rules that are necessary to preserve the atmosphere of the library.

When discipline measures are necessary, the librarian must handle them himself rather than rely on the classroom teacher, though there is seldom any harm in discussing the matter with the teacher. The measures the librarian chooses to use must be within the framework of the school's policies and, when possible, should not deny the child the right to use the library facilities that are necessary to his educational and personal growth. Suspension from all privileges should be considered only when a situation has reached the point where it is no longer possible to preserve the atmosphere of the library or to maintain a good teaching situation.

Grading the Instructional Program

Some school systems require the instructional program in the library to be graded on the children's report card in the same as other class activities. Such a requirement may be unfair to the child.

The library instruction class is not held for the sake of the library, but to enable the children to acquire skills and knowledge that will help them achieve a higher level of performance in other areas of the school curriculum, or to help satisfy some personal interest or need. The personal value a child receives from a particular book or other library item is virtually impossible to grade. The skills and knowledge he acquires in the library program are probably better graded in those curriculum areas where they are needed and used.

The librarian's teaching time is short, he is likely to set few or no tests, and at the end of a grading period he will not have gathered a sufficient number of scores to average into an accurate description of the child's performance. The result, if he has to grade students, is likely to be a somewhat perfunctory grade which is not descriptive of the child's actual accomplishment, and is hardly fair to him.

Occasionally, in an effort to accumulate more scores in order to arrive at a more accurate, descriptive grade, it is suggested that the librarian include the quantity of materials charged by the children, the number of overdue items and lost or damaged materials. It is not realistic to assign a grade on the quantity of materials a child may charge, for the librarian has no way of knowing what value the child received from the titles. The children soon discover when this system is applied in grading and some will charge a large amount of material for which they have little need or interest. Though the librarian records the daily circulation, to require him to keep a record of the materials charged to each individual burdens him with an unnecessary clerical task or requires the employment of additional personnel to keep such records. It also results in amassing a body of information which probably serves no useful purpose in most library situations.

Overdue materials, damage and similar problems occur with greater frequency with some individuals than with others. These are largely discipline problems, the result of attitudes and habits, none of which are solved by the threat of poor grades. There will always be some tardiness in returns and some damaged or lost materials in any library. When these are excessive, the librarian needs to seek the causes rather than lower grades on a report card.

There may be psychological reasons, too, for not grading the library instructional program. The children are under constant pressure to achieve at acceptable levels, pressures almost always exerted by parents, teachers, the child's peers, or other sources outside the child himself. Acceptable levels of performance are all too often based on comparative criteria which do not consider the child as an individual, and which may force him to attempt goals that, for him, may be impractical.

The library may be one area in the school environment where the child can work without these pressures, a refuge where he can work for himself. Here, he could literally grade himself when he discovers that his work in other classes is made easier because of the skills he has acquired in the library.

The librarian who is asked to grade children in the library instruction program is faced with a difficult problem.

He must do it as well as he can while being as fair as possible to the children, but he should also seek a solution to the problem through his administrator. An administrator who is looking for ways to avoid the traditional grading system in the school may find it advantageous to begin by abandoning grades in the library program.

Field Trips

Occasional field trips to other libraries, research centers, museums or publishing houses are desirable. Such excursions must always be planned within the framework of the school's policies, and should include good preparation and follow-up activities.

Nonprofessional, Volunteer Assistance

Assistance offered by organizations such as the Parent-Teacher's Association can be a real help to the busy librarian and can contribute to the library program, its publicity and community relations. Such activities as library teas, clerical assistance and help with visitation days are examples. There may be a place in the instructional program of the library for some of these people to engage in occasional story telling or assist in the preparation of instructional materials. Such assistance should only be considered if there is a real need these people can fill; and they must be qualified or willing to accept training. Perhaps of most importance, their duties and responsibilities should be clearly spelled out, in order to prevent any individual or group from becoming so involved that they assume duties or responsibilities that rightfully belong to the professional librarian, or that they usurp the librarian's authority and right to final decisions.

Financing the Instructional Program

Financing the instructional program in the library should present no particular problem since the materials and equipment used are those already in the library or available from general school supplies. Where a librarian does elect to use commercially prepared materials, the cost, when pro-rated over the several years of expected life, is usually nominal.

Commercially prepared materials, film rentals and other costs of the program should not be charged against the library materials budget which is designed to provide the printed materials, audio-visual aids and other instructional tools used by the children and teachers throughout the areas of the school curriculum. Where it is found advisable to place instructional costs into the library budget, these costs should appear separately and additional funds should be provided, so that the normal funds for material acquisition and maintenance are not reduced as a result.

Other areas of library administration, such as charging fines and the treatment of lost or damaged materials, may affect the instructional program. However, they are more closely related to the general administration of the library and a discussion of them here would serve little purpose.

Chapter 3

The Library Instructional Program in the Kindergarten

The library is confronted with what is probably both its greatest opportunity and its greatest responsibility in the kindergarten. Many of the youngsters starting school may be experiencing their first encounter with books, pictures, and the other varied and interesting materials housed in the library, as well as with the pleasant, friendly environment of the library. It is of the utmost importance that these children find this experience both pleasurable and personally satisfying to insure a sound beginning of a desirable life-long attitude toward books, libraries and knowledge itself.

To help meet this objective in the library instructional program, emphasis is placed on story telling, sharing, browsing, and some very elementary research. A few basic rules necessary to library operation are also discussed and gently enforced.

Story Telling

Though the purpose of this book is not to offer instruction in the story telling art, the activity is of so much importance, and so much of the kindergarten's library time is spent in this area, that a brief discussion of some of the more successful methods is pertinent.

The direct method of story telling is perhaps the most common. The story-teller gathers the children around him and shows the illustrations in the book as he reads the story.

Mrs. Jaggers reads a story to
a group of her youngsters.

The group is very informal, the children usually seated on cushions on the floor, while the story teller uses a low stool. The story can be interrupted for a comment or question without destroying the effect, and the children are easily made aware that the story is coming from the book; an association that is not always apparent to very young children.

An interesting variation, which can work well when a group is quite large, or when a change in method or presentation is desired, involves the use of an opaque projector in the same setting as the story telling. The book is placed in the projector and the enlarged illustration focused onto a screen or a blank wall. The story teller reads the story as each page appears on the screen. There are several disadvantages to this method, the principle ones being the necessity of darkening the room, and the handling problem--since the elevator must be dropped, the page turned, and the elevator again positioned whenever the story teller reaches the end of a page. This procedure is distracting and interrupts the story. The handling problem can be alleviated by cutting the needed illustrations from a discarded copy of the story (two copies are usually needed), mounting these pages on a continuous strip of paper, and simply rolling the strip with its mounted pictures through the projector as they are needed.

Older students with a liking and flair for art may prepare drawings for one or two of the children's stories; the youngsters particularly enjoy stories told to their own illustrations.

In spite of its disadvantages, this method of story presentation does allow for a greatly enlarged picture, considerable interest and attention is generated by the hardware, and the lighted screen, in sharp contrast to the darkened room is a powerful attractor. Though the method would not be desirable if used too frequently, it does offer a change in presentation and a defense against possible boredom created by too much "sameness" in the story hour.

A somewhat similar method of presentation uses the TV or movie screen box with which all teachers are familiar. Children's illustrations or pictures cut from discarded books are mounted on a long strip of paper and either pulled across the viewing side of the box or rolled on dowels which have been built into the box for this purpose. Usually some form of illumination is required. A goose-neck lamp shining on the screen, or, if the paper and pictures have been painted with shellac to make them transparent, a light placed behind the opening and allowed to shine through the paper will prove quite satisfactory. Narration may be added to each illustration and read, the story may be told as the illustrations appear, or the narration may be placed on tape.

Another effective method uses oversized, free-standing pictures illustrating the main incidents of the story. These are arranged about the story teller in sequential order and are indicated as the story progresses. These pictures can be made quite durable and not too difficult to store, and they have the added advantage of being usable for library decoration, book display and advertising. Classroom teachers may borrow some of them to use in working with sequence in their reading classes.

That this method is not used more often is because most librarians do not have time to prepare the pictures. They can, however, quite easily be done by an older student or a "friend" of the library. The book illustration is placed in an opaque projector, enlarged to the required size, and then traced. Decoration can be completed in any art medium that is desired. Though it takes time to prepare these illustrations, the results of this technique can be well worth the effort.

A variation of this method involves the children more directly, with each one selecting an incident from the story, preparing his own illustration and taking his part in a group re-telling of the story. The classroom teacher may find this activity sufficiently rewarding to give class time, and it works well as a contribution to a school program when the illustrations are done on paper large enough to be seen easily by an audience.

There are some interesting indirect methods of story telling, one of which involves the use of hand puppets. These can be purchased or made. The story selected to be told by the puppets must be quite simple, and must use a very limited number of characters so that the puppets can be handled smoothly and quickly. More than one person may be involved in the story telling, and some sort of staging may be used, though this is not essential. The method requires some practice, since the story-teller should be adept at handling the puppets, and voice changes to fit the characters are desirable. A great deal of showmanship must go into the production if it is to succeed, but when well done, this approach is very effective.

Simply to have a hand puppet through which a story is told may not, however, be effective for long because the puppet remains just a puppet telling a story, and the children soon loose interest in the novelty of the presentation. The cloth and plastic puppet simply cannot substitute for a warm, understanding human friend who tells an interesting story.

Film strips, either narrated by the story teller or accompanied by a record or tape, are always interesting and many of these are well done, as are the available 16 mm educational films. There are also a great number of children's story records available at low cost, and children may bring some from home for sharing. When using any of these methods of story telling, the librarian needs to preview the material carefully to be certain that the story has not suffered in adaptation, that the particular version is satisfactory, and that the material is well read.

The main caution in using indirect methods of story telling is that this technique takes the story away from the book, and some children may fail to associate the story with the printed page.

The Story Teller

Most librarians, through experience and training, are accomplished tellers of stories and generally assume the major role in this activity. The classroom teacher may also be adept at the art and there is no reason why she, too, should not assume some of the pleasures of this activity should she be willing to do so.

There may be individuals among such "friends" of the library as the Parent-Teacher's Association or the local Women's Club who are both capable and willing to contribute some of their time to this part of the library instructional program. Older children, particularly those who are Student Librarians or members of the Library Club should not be overlooked in the search for new faces. With some training, intelligent students often become quite adept at story telling and the experience may give them an added incentive to pursue teaching or library work as a profession.

One of the greatest experiences the children can have in the library is a visit by one of the authors of children's books. Since these people keep busy schedules, and some form of honorarium is customary, scheduling such library activities becomes an excellent project for the Library Committee of the Parent-Teacher's Association or one of the other civic organizations in the community.

Whoever tells the story, and whatever method is used, the story teller must be an accomplished reader, and able to associate with the age group before him or the results are likely to be something less than desired, and the experience may contribute little toward the objective of the story hour.

Selection Criteria for the Story Hour

A list of criteria for story hour selection could be nearly endless, and still not fit all schools and all situations. Yet, observation demonstrates four points that, probably because of lack of time, are occasionally neglected by both librarians and teachers.

1. The story must be within the attention span of the group for which it is intended. The story teller must be aware of the reception, and prepared to adjust the time if necessary. It would appear that eight to ten minutes for the kindergarten and primary grades is about maximum.
2. The theme, vocabulary, interest and concepts must be within the ability of the age group to comprehend. With some groups, such as those encountered in the Head Start Programs, the cultural levels of the children may be even more important than their maturity level, and must be considered.
3. The story must not obviously preach or lecture. Socio-drama and similar techniques are probably best

left to the classroom unless the teacher has specifically requested such a procedure and has planned with the librarian well ahead of the scheduled class period. At best, such activity can be hazardous for the librarian and should be avoided when possible.

4. The story should be one which the story teller enjoys. This always makes the story more interesting, and is more satisfying to both the children and the story teller.

Browsing

Browsing is the second principle activity of the library period, and if it is not to be a frustrating exercise there must be an adequate collection of large and small picture books from which to choose. There should also be flat pictures, models and items of realia which the children can handle.

The children should be allowed to take some of this material back to their classroom, though charging material for home use at this age is a matter of individual library policy. At Clearlake Oaks, such material is charged from the library for school use, and taking the material home is left to the discretion of the teacher since she is much better acquainted with the individual children and their homes. The children are encouraged to use the public library facilities for their "take-home" selections.

Sharing

In the classroom, sharing is a talking and showing time during which a child may describe a recent vacation trip, show a favorite doll, or tell about the operation on his puppy. In the library, sharing is related to the books and

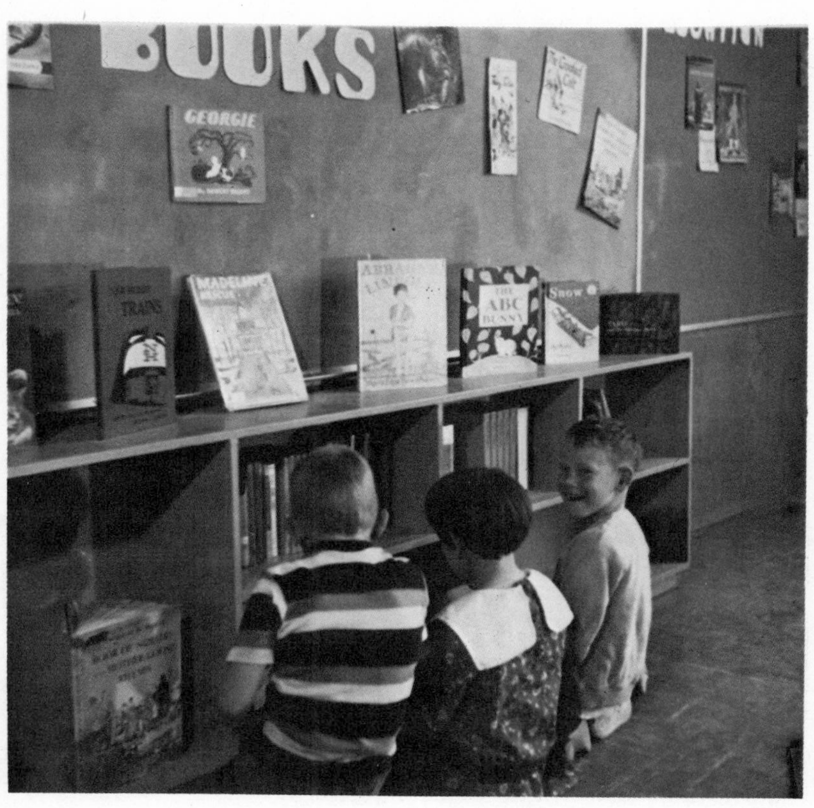

Browsing is not always an individualized activity.

materials themselves, and includes such things as sharing an experience similar to one encountered in a story, telling an original story, or discussing a question such as, "What might happen if-----?" or "How do you think the story will end?" Occasionally this sharing and talking activity is planned, but often it will be a spontaneous outburst of comment. In such cases the librarian should provide sufficient direction to prevent rambling, monopolizing, or the injection of unrelated topics.

Rules of the Library

A few simple rules need to be discussed and kept in constant review. Whatever rules the librarian uses, they must be kept to only the minimum necessary to reach the desired objectives, and should be introduced with free discussion and, when possible, some dramatization. It helps if the classroom teacher will take a moment or two each time the class lines up to come to the library, to briefly review these rules. Constant reminder and gentle individual discussion when necessary, coupled with good management, should help build these rules into habit.

Experience at Clearlake Oaks has shown the universal rule of "quiet" to be the most difficult to build into habit. To be quiet is against young children's natural inclinations, yet it must be achieved to a degree consistent with the maturity levels. There will be some noisy sharing during the browsing portion of the period, and enthusiasm will occasionally bubble over. Some of this can be, and should be, ignored. Individual reminders should be given when necessary, and it is helpful if the younger children have an opportunity to see older children using the library in a quiet and orderly manner. If further enforcement proves necessary, it must be handled firmly, decisively and consistently, but always with a gentleness which preserves, as far as possible, the friendly posture of the library.

Another rule that can sometimes prove troublesome concerns the disposition of material which has been removed from the shelves but which is not going to be charged from the library. A convenient shelf or table may be used for a depository, but the best solution is a shallow, brightly colored box. If a cardboard carton is used, it need cost the library nothing. This box may be decorated with a seasonal theme, holiday decoration, original designs, or may serve as a bulletin board. The box should be conveniently located but out of the main lines of traffic. Material may be easily re-shelved from the box.

The librarian should not forget to include an occasional fire drill since it is unlikely that such drills will occur during the library periods unless the librarian has made such a request of the administration. A good time for a planned fire drill is at the close of the period when the children, excited by the occasion, will not be expected to return to the quiet activity of the library.

Such general rules as having clean hands, not to eat while reading, how to turn a page and carry a book are handled through frequent discussions and demonstrations, as are other rules the librarian may find it necessary to introduce at this grade level.

Elementary Research

The children must learn as early as possible that the library is a source of information as well as a source of interesting materials. Close cooperation between the classroom teacher and the librarian is required if this is to be achieved, for most of the opportunities to use the library for research will emanate from the classroom.

When a butterfly is brought to school and the children want to know what kind it is, they might bring it to the library where the librarian will help with identification by picture comparisons. When a little boy does not know what a dragon fly looks like, he should be sent to the library for help in locating a picture of the insect, or to examine a mounted specimen from the library collection. Countless such opportunities to use the library will occur and a good many of these should be utilized if the children are to develop the habit of relying on the library as a source of information, and are to recognize the library facilities as an extension of their own classroom.

Whatever activities are presented in the library instructional program for the Kindergarten, and however they are organized, there must be one principle objective: to present an environment which will instill in the child a love of good materials and the recognition of the library as a friendly, helpful place to browse and work. Unless the library is successful in this objective, all activities become somewhat pointless, for the child will at best be a reluctant user of library facilities.

Chapter 4

The Program in the First Grade

The library instructional program for the first grade is largely an extension of the objectives and methods used in the kindergarten, with continued emphasis being placed on story telling, browsing, research, sharing, and developing the few necessary rules into habit.

During the second half of the year the children will learn to identify the covers and spines of a book, and will practice their alphabet by reading the call numbers on the spines of the E books. The children will also be introduced to the easy picture dictionaries.

The Covers and Spine of the Book

The children learn to identify the covers and spine of a book through a somewhat incidental activity in the classroom. Their work papers, art and other classroom efforts are periodically gathered together and made into booklets to be sent home. The children select the colored construction paper they want to use to make the "covers" for their booklets. When the papers are all in place, the teacher, or librarian, helps them staple their booklets along the "spine." This method of instruction has proven at Clearlake Oaks to be the most productive in achieving early and easy use of these two terms.

When the children have added these terms to their speaking vocabulary, they may be allowed to observe a demonstration of simple book repair involving the covers and spine. This activity serves to point out the damage which can result from wear or from careless handling and provides the librarian with an opportunity to use the terms cover and spine in a different context.

It might appear that simply holding up a book and telling the children that "this is the spine and these are the covers" would be sufficient. Experience has shown, however, that without the associated activity only a small percentage of the children at this age will incorporate the two terms easily and naturally into their vocabulary.

Working with the Alphabet

Once the children have a fair mastery of the alphabet, they may begin reading the letters of the call numbers in the E section of the library. At first, the children practice reading the call numbers on the books they are charging to their classroom (Individualized instruction). They will soon notice that all the call numbers begin with an E. When they ask about this, the librarian should explain that the E tells them the book or other item is for their own grade level, and also tells the librarian where to shelve the books.

When most of the children are able to read the letters easily they should walk along the shelves and notice the alphabetical arrangement of the books. A simple game may now be played. Two children are asked to locate a certain shelf when the teacher or librarian gives them a call number. The children walk to the shelf, and the first one to point this out wins. The winner has the opportunity of selecting the next person to play. The loser may play again, and in this way, gain additional practice.

In those few libraries where the E section is fully

cataloged and shelved with the regular collection, it is best to use only the fiction section in playing this game. Older children, who have had more experience with retrieval and who are comfortable with numbers, will play more sophisticated games.

Most children enjoy this kind of game in the library, but it also gives them practice in developing fluency with the alphabet, helps them begin to understand the organization of a library, and may contribute to the development of proper left-to-right progression so common in their other school activities.

The Picture Dictionary

The dictionary may be introduced by the librarian in the library, or by the teacher in the classroom. In either case the technique of instruction will probably be the same. The librarian or teacher holds up a picture dictionary and announces to the class that this is a very special and interesting book. A few pages should be flipped so that the children can see the pictures. The children are told that this is a book of words, and other copies, which have been previously arranged on a convenient shelf or table, are pointed out to them. It is suggested that they might like to charge one for browsing.

Following this introduction, the children are asked what they thought of the dictionary, and such questions as, "Did you find the pictures interesting?" and "Did you find any words you knew?" The children are then asked if they know what kind of a book this is, or what it is called. Some little "sharpie" may recall that you have used the word dictionary, and some children will probably know the term and contribute it to the discussion. If there are none who will give this information, then they should be told that this book is called the dictionary and that it is arranged like the library shelves; all the A's are together, the B's are together, and so on through the alphabet. It should be suggested that the next time they encounter a word they do not know, they might try to find it in one of the picture dictionaries and discover its meaning.

Since the greatest opportunity for use occurs in the classroom, the teacher should use every opportunity to encourage the children to make use of this tool, even though she may have to give a great deal of individual assistance at first. She can, of course, occasionally send the child to the library for such help.

Though teachers and librarians may find a class now and then that is ready to go beyond this bare introduction to the dictionary, and will probably do so, achieving maximum utility of this reference tool is apt to be a long and sometimes arduous process for many children, and the initial introduction must be pleasant if it is to have any chance of being successful. There is little to be gained by forcing use of the dictionary before there is an actual need, or before the child has sufficient educational maturity properly to apply the skills necessary to use this important tool easily.

In teaching use of the dictionary or other skills, it is most important that the librarian work closely with the classroom teacher. Various textbooks have units of work which deal with reference tools, and joint planning will prevent duplication of effort. Such cooperation also helps to prevent any possible feeling by one party that the other is usurping some part of his responsibilities. It may seem that professional people should not become embroiled in an argument of this nature, but it does happen, and the responsibility for its prevention, in relation to the library teaching program, rests squarely with the librarian's willingness to accept leadership in the development of the spirit of cooperation. The important issue is not, and should not be, who is going to teach the material. That it is taught, and taught well, should be the only consideration.

The librarian should find that the suggestions offered here, combined with a large amount of story time, browsing and sharing as outlined in the chapter dealing with the kindergarten, will completely fill the year's alloted time. If the librarian can maintain and further develop the desirable attitudes toward books and libraries that were begun in the kindergarten, and can develop in the children a good understanding of the alphabet in the organization of the E section of the library, he will have accomplished his basic objectives for this grade level.

Book Selection

Before leaving the first grade, there is one matter of book selection in the primary grades that is worth note. It sometimes happens that these younger children wander off into other sections of the library, and select titles which are much too difficult for them. This writer is of the opinion that the difficulty of a title should be pointed out to a child, but that if he remains insistent and an easier title on the same subject does not prove interesting, he should be allowed to charge out the title and discover for himself that he is not yet able to read it. The librarian can never be sure just what a child "gets out of a book." Though the title may be too difficult, the child may still find something in the illustrations which proves most satisfying.

Chapter 5

The Program in the Second Grade

The library instructional program in the second grade is essentially the same as that presented in the kindergarten and the first grade, with the story hour, sharing, browsing and some elementary research consuming the major portion of the library time. There is also a continuing effort to develop into habit the few necessary rules of the library. Work with the dictionary is continued and the term "Title Page" is added to the children's library vocabulary.

The Story Hour

The story hour should include, in addition to interesting and seasonal stories, some poetry, an occasional short drama the children may read in parts or walk through, and some simple jokes, humorous stories and cartoons. A story now and then from one of the children's magazines is also desirable.

A portion of the story hour should be given over to the children to talk about things they have read, or about television and movie programs. At least once during the year, each child should have the opportunity to share something through the use of the tape recorder. These talks may also be used for book reports by those teachers who may require this activity of their children, and the teacher may like to have the children write their talks in the classroom before taping them in the library.

Sharing is also an aid to book selection
at all grade levels.

The principal objective of this library activity is not necessarily to develop excellence in oral presentation, but to give each child some opportunity to develop a comfortable attitude before a group of friends, and to help bring each child into contact with as many materials as possible. Very little corrective comment should be made on the delivery other than to keep the talks brief and in proper sequence. No situation which might embarrass the young speaker should ever be tolerated. It is the responsibility of the professional person conducting the class to do everything possible to make each talk a satisfying experience both for the child sharing his story and for the young listeners.

The tape recorder should not be introduced to the children as a means of sharing good stories until they have had an opportunity to experience its use as a class group. It is best if the teacher can find use for the hardware in the classroom, to tape a song the children are singing, or perhaps to tape one of their plays as a vehicle for discussing ways to improve their production. When this isn't possible, the librarian should use a taped presentation of a story and allow the children to "play" with the equipment, giving at least some of them an opportunity to say something into the microphone and to hear the play-back. What is put on the tape at such times is of little importance. The objective is to acquaint the children with the machine and thus reduce "mike-fright". To force any child to present his talk on the recorder may be unwise. Both mike fright and stage fright can be very devastating for some children and forcing them to use the equipment will accomplish little toward helping them gain confidence in themselves.

When a child is ready to tape his talk, he should go into the conference room or office where the equipment is located. The teacher or librarian must be the operator. Some schools use student technicians, but these young aids should not be used here, for this is a teaching situation where a child will often need help, advice and encouragement. Where there is some reluctance on the part of the child, the presence of someone he knows and trusts will help give him the confidence he needs to produce a creditable talk.

The taped report should always be played back during the same class period in which it is recorded. Most children, contrary to some of their protestations, are very anxious to hear their tape, and too long a time lapse between recording and play-back can be disappointing to the child and may result in a loss of interest in the technique.

The tape recorder is an excellent means of presenting at least some of the reports children are required to do throughout their school years, and an early introduction to the method is desirable.

Though the story teller, using varied techniques in the practice of his art will use much of the available time himself, he should, as the year progresses, gradually give an increased amount of time to the children for sharing and talking about the good things they have read and heard.

The Title Page

During the first grade, the children's library vocabulary was expanded to include the terms "covers" and "spine". In the second grade the "title page" is introduced.

Talking about the title page is necessary as an introduction, but this alone will not put the term into the children's working vocabulary. Writing original stories is a part of every classroom's activity, and this offers the opportunity to use a title page. Though the stories these youngsters write are usually very short, they should be illustrated, placed into covers, and a title page added. This page should include the title, the young author's name, the date (substitution for copyright date), and the school as the place of publication. Though much of this work will be done in the classroom, there is no reason why it cannot also be done, on occasion, in the library. When sharing their completed stories, the children should be encouraged to share their title pages too.

One teacher felt that the publisher should be included on the title page. To accomplish this, and to facilitate some of her own work, she set up a publishing company in her classroom. The company consisted of a small group of students who stapled the children's pages into the covers after checking them for completeness. They also added the publishing company's name to each title page.

Each spring the library at Clearlake Oaks holds a tea for the school and general public. The tea features the art, construction, language and other classroom projects which relate to the library and its services. The stories of these young authors always receive feature display, and are examined with a great deal of interest by the guests.

Though discussion, demonstration and other methods have been used, early introduction of the title page, using the above outlined activity method as a major part of the presentation, has proven the most effective approach.

The Dictionary

Work with the dictionary at this grade level is concerned with the development of first letter alphabetization and introduction to the guide words.

The work begins with a review of the alphabet and with the shelf arrangement of the books in the E section. The children are then introduced to an easy game. Some large cards, each marked with a different call number and including the whole alphabet, have been prepared beforehand by members of the library club or the student librarians. Three children take their make-believe books (cards) to the front of the group and arrange themselves in alphabetical order. The class may help with this. Another child is then called on to go up with his card and position himself in such a way as to preserve the alphabetical order. If he does this correctly, he then calls on another student to come up and try with his card. If he misses, he is either helped by the class and loses the right to call on another student, or he may trade cards with someone and observe his card being placed in the proper position. He then tries again with his new card. The game continues until all the children are standing, or until five or six people have played, when a new game is started.

The teacher or coach may also use these cards in a relay game. Here each team member is given a card, and one card is placed on the ground before each team. Each member runs forward, places his card in such a manner as to preserve the alphabetical order (which is checked and corrected when necessary before the child returns to his team), then tags the next member who repeats the process. The first team to complete all its cards wins the relay game.

The children are now given words to look up in their picture dictionaries. The words to be used should be those selected by the classroom teacher, and should be checked to be certain they are included in the dictionaries being used. The first word is printed on a large card and placed before the class. The children first read the word, and then are asked to find the page number on which they find this word. Though some of the children will recognize the alphabetical arrangement and will go directly to the correct section of the dictionary, others will begin by leafing through the book at random, hoping to locate the word. Once the word has been found, the spelling and definitions should be pointed out to the class. This procedure should be used with the next two or three words. Then the librarian should point out the first letter of the ~~next~~ word, and ask its relative position in the alphabet--near the front, in the middle, or close to the back? It can be pointed out to the children that since the dictionary is arranged in alphabetical order, the word will be found in the corresponding part of the book. The children are asked to try to open their dictionaries to the section which contains those words beginning with the same letter as the word on the printed card. This activity should be encouraged, both in the library and classroom, until the children discover that it is not necessary to begin in the "A" section when they are looking for a word that begins with "S".

The librarian and teacher need to circulate among the group as this search is going on. The classroom teacher will probably give added practice in the classroom, and individual help to any student having difficulty.

The guide words are pointed out and used as an aid in locating the correct section of the dictionary. Refining the children's skills in using the guide words is perhaps most successful when done by the classroom teacher in her own room where there is more need during the day for use of the dictionary. The same is true of the rules for spelling and phonics.

Elementary Research

The research work done in the kindergarten and first grade is continued in the second with little change. The classroom teacher should continue using opportunities to send children to the library for such research, for only in this way will the children come to recognize the library as a source of information and an aid to their classroom and personal work. To develop the habit of depending upon the library for this type of work is a vital objective of the library program in the elementary school.

When the children have completed their research, they may be asked to present their findings to the class. This may necessitate the charging of books, pictures, models, film strips or other materials available to the children from the library collection. Thus it provides a way to acquaint them with the wide range of materials, and offers a good start in the research and reporting that will be formalized in the later school years.

Though the librarian may need to teach different materials or adjust the depth of the work in his own particular school from what has been suggested here, his principle objective must be to present a program and environment that will help the child both enjoy the library experience and come to recognize the library as a valuable tool toward the accomplishment of his own personal and educational goals.

Chapter 6

The Program in the Third Grade

The library instruction in the third grade is largely a further extension of the activities in the other primary grades, with emphasis on broadening the children's interests and the variety of materials they select. They are also introduced to an easier encyclopedia and an atlas, and to charging materials for their own use.

Charging Materials

Since there are a variety of charging methods in libraries, it is not possible to describe any single method which will be acceptable to all libraries. Libraries also differ in the age groups they allow to charge out materials for home use. However, whatever method of charging is used, and no matter the age, some form of activity method for teaching the charging of materials will probably prove to be the most effective.

At Clearlake Oaks a very simple charge card is used. The card contains the call number, copy number, author's name and title, and has space for the children to sign their name and grade, and for the date due stamp. These blank cards are ordered from a library supply house and are typed at the time of processing.

The children are first shown a transparency of a charge card that contains the title identification but is otherwise blank. This information is discussed, and any questions are answered. Then the librarian adds a student's name, the first name and last initial, and his grade to the card. He then stamps the date due on the card. A library in an ungraded school, instead of using a grade designation, might use the teacher's initials. The children observe this process and ask questions about it. Care should be taken to explain the reasons for this method of signature.

When this has been done, two or three children write their names and grade on the transparency, and the librarian adds the date due with the dater.

The children are then given a ditto work sheet containing a duplicate of the transparency, and each is asked to complete the charge card properly. The teacher and librarian move among the group, checking their work and offering any assistance that might be needed. The date due is calculated by the class, and they use a dater to stamp this information on the ditto sheets.

When the children are charging their books, each card is carefully checked for accuracy at the desk, and should a mistake occur, the child is sent to the teacher or clerk to make corrections and any additional necessary explanation or practice is given. This checking for accuracy in completion of the charge card is a continuous activity of the student librarians or clerks who are instructed not to charge materials improperly signed.

Audio-visual materials, items from the vertical file and periodicals do not have charge cards with them. These are charged on a charge slip kept at the desk. In the case of audio-visual materials, there is usually no convenient place to affix a pocket and card, and magazines and other periodicals are frequently designed so that the placement of a pocket may obliterate some of the material. Also, some of this material is ephemeral and may not remain in circulation long enough to warrant the cost of a regular charge card and its preparation. The charging of this special material is taught by the same methods as used with regular circulations.

Instruction in the charging method is followed by the rules governing this library operation. Discussion methods work well, but should be supplemented by ditto copies of the rules which each child can have in hand during the discussion. Care must be taken to explain the "why" for each rule, and to answer carefully any questions the children may ask. These rules must be strictly enforced with the least number of "exceptions" possible.

No attempt is made here to suggest charging regulations since this is an administrative problem within each school. No matter what rules and regulations may be in force, the teaching method will probably remain the same.

The Story Hour

Though the reading and sharing of stories is continued in the third grade, more time is spent in talking about books, and "selling" different types of material. The children in the third grade are developing reading skills and interests that will take many of them out of the E section of the library, and they need to be made aware of the many subjects available to them.

The music teacher would probably welcome the opportunity to visit one of the library periods and read an adapted version of one of the operas, or a story like "Peter and the Wolf," or play a few selections from the title. Simple books on magic, art techniques and special hobbies may also be handled similarly through such guest visits.

Simple walk-through drama, poetry, cook books, party and game titles, biography and other materials from the wide variety in the library collection should be introduced. Reading, telling and showing are only three of the methods that may be used. Book display, bulletin boards, book reports and, all-important, individual guidance must not be neglected as methods of selling materials.

Some of the material used during the story hour should come from the library magazines and story records, and should also include materials available to the children from the public library and any special libraries which may be in the area. Even a circulating museum should not be overlooked.

Reporting

The work in reporting and individual story writing and telling which was started in the second grade should be continued as a joint effort of the library and classroom. When doing this work, the librarian should introduce the children to sources of information about the author and illustrator, and should encourage the children to include a very short statement about these people. When a picture of the author or illustrator is available, often on the dust jacket, the children should be allowed to show this as a part of their report.

Shelf Arrangement

Shelving games similar to those introduced in the second grade should be continued. These are fun for the children if they are not overdone and they offer an excellent readiness program for the more detailed work that comes in the fourth and fifth grades.

The Dictionary

Much of the work with the dictionary will be handled in the regular classroom during the formalized language and social studies instruction. When words are encountered that are not in the children's dictionaries, the children may be sent to the library to use the larger editions, including the unabridged dictionary which they all love. The librarian must help the children in using these tools because of their more difficult language. The assistance provided by the librarian should include using the guide words, locating the proper definition or spelling, and using the thumb tabs. The child should always be able to observe the librarian using aids in location, and must be made to feel free to ask questions. A question will sometimes arise in the classroom which presents an opportunity to use one of the special sections found in the unabridged dictionary, and the wise teacher will utilize these opportunities to the full.

The method of teaching the use of the dictionary presented here may appear to be incidental and casual. However, the librarian cannot teach everything and good formal instruction is offered in the classroom. This suggested method takes advantage of the actual needs of the children at the most opportune moment, and, since such situations occur throughout the year there is more continuous instruction in use of the dictionary than there would be if a block of time where simply assigned for this work, and all children were "taught" to use the dictionary properly and efficiently at this time. The educational process would be greatly simplified if "teaching" could be so neatly arranged.

Fortunately, at Clearlake Oaks, there have been good teaching practices which are cognizant of the role of the library and its staff as ready adjuncts to the work of the classroom. In less desirable situations the librarian may need to present a more complete program of instruction in the use of the dictionary.

The librarian will find, as the children progress through school, that while he has a block of time to be used in library instruction, he will probably be doing as much teaching during other periods when individuals and small groups come to the library to seek information, to browse, or sometimes just to escape for a few minutes the sights and sounds of the classroom environment.

Chapter 7

The Program in the Fourth Grade

The fourth grade year should begin with a review of the charging rules and procedures as well as a review of the general rules of the library. When this is completed, the children should begin work aimed at developing skills in locating specific materials in the library collection, and a large share of the librarian's instructional time will be spent in activities designed to build these skills. The story hour is continued, though it should not demand as much of the librarian's time as in the lower grades. Good literature is told and shared, but an increasing portion of the activity will be devoted to discussing different types of materials, and to selling these materials as an aid in broadening the children's interests.

Shelf Arrangement

When the review has been completed, and this should consume comparatively little of the librarian's instructional time, a detailed study of the shelf arrangement should be undertaken.

The first activity is a guided tour of the shelves. The class should be divided into as many small groups as possible. During this tour, the shelving is explained, and the librarian will use such library terms as "shelf," "stack" and "range." The librarian must be careful to point out the alphabetical arrangement of the fiction section and the alphabetical arrangement within the numbers in the nonfiction collection.

Following the tour of the library, a ditto floor plan of the library showing the shelf arrangement is given to each child. Each child moves along the ranges with his floor plan, filling in the call numbers as he comes to them. This activity requires some time, and some of the children will need assistance with the work, but it places each child in a position where he must actually look at the call numbers and read them. Simply discussing the shelf arrangement will not prove successful.

Once the map has been completed, the children enjoy game activities for practice in shelf arrangement. One game is played by giving two children call numbers, and then asking them to walk to the shelves and locate a book with that call number. The first one to locate a title wins, and chooses someone else to race the loser. A variation of the game allows the loser to challenge someone else to race. Having the winner retire from the game offers some assurance that the loser will gain added practice.

When first using the game, only general call numbers should be used, such as asking for a title from the JH shelf, or a title from the 500 shelf. As the children gain experience, specific call numbers may be given. The children should never be given the same call number, or they may collide on their way to the shelf or argue over who arrived first. There is also danger that the weaker child would simply follow the lead of the other instead of depending upon himself. The same game is played when the children are practicing retrieving specific titles, titles dealing with specific subjects, or titles by a given author.

Another excellent activity, which aids in shelf location, is to have the children actually shelve materials. This is not done to save work for the library staff but to offer additional practice in shelf location. Each child is given a title to shelve. He does so, and then stands with his finger on the material until its location is checked. When a mistake is made in shelving, assistance is given in locating the proper shelf.

If the children are to develop confidence in retrieving materials, they must know where materials are shelved or stored, and these game activities, periodically repeated throughout the year, will do much to assist the development of this library skill.

Spine Markings

While the children are learning shelf location, they should also be learning the meanings of the spine markings. This work was accomplished for several years at Clearlake Oaks by the use of transparencies, ditto sheets, discussions, demonstrations and question-answer methods. A search for a less time-consuming method led to the development of a programmed instruction booklet.

The booklet, included in Appendix A, underwent eleven revisions and twelve testing procedures before it proved successful, but its success and saving in time has made the labor worthwhile. The program is presented here for any librarian to use, though adjustments in some of the frames may be necessary where there are differences in library cataloging procedures. Once the work with spine markings is completed it should be kept in review by an occasional game or short period of questions and answers.

At Clearlake Oaks, the audio-visual materials are

stored in areas separated from the shelved collection and are cataloged in book form using title entries and subject heading entries. The location of this material is taught through discussion and demonstration techniques and an occasional locating game.

The Card Catalog

Some children will have been using the card catalog before they have reached the fourth grade, and some librarians have begun such instruction in the lower grades. It has been found at Clearlake Oaks that work with the card catalog in the primary grades meets with only partial success, and must be reintroduced at the fourth grade level. It appears best to wait until most of the children have gained sufficient maturity to work comfortably with the required skills, and have more actual need for this library tool.

For several years, oversized flip cards were used to teach use of catalog cards. These were designed so that the needed portion of the card could be flipped into view as it was needed. Though the method proved quite satisfactory, transparencies of the cards are now used because storage of the cards presented a problem, and they had to be re-made now and then to preserve their fresh appearance. The transparencies thus save both time and money and the hardware seems to have an attraction itself which leads to better attention.

Bulletin board display of cards has been found to be very helpful when used in conjunction with this unit of work, and has served as a useful tool in reviewing catalog use with older children. The small poster notes of explanation, such as those available from library supply houses, have proven to be a waste of funds and space, either as an initial teaching tool or for review purposes.

Since the subject card is the one most frequently used by the children, it is the first to be introduced. Analytics are handled as subject headings since the children use both for the same purpose. The analytic card is discussed only when some child notices that one card is in capital letters, and another in lower case. A simple explanation is usually sufficient to satisfy the children.

The initial transparency contains only a subject heading. HORSES - STORIES is used because the subject is always popular with the children. The question, "Why is this called a 'Subject Card'?" will usually develop a correct response, though some guesswork and leading questions may be necessary before a satisfactory answer is given.

The second transparency contains the heading and a call number. This is discussed in the same way as the subject heading, though it usually requires only a few moments since the children have been working with these in their shelving activities. The next transparency adds the author and title. After a discussion on these entries, the children should be asked if they could locate the book on the shelves, and someone is selected to do this.

At this point the librarian may find it desirable to write several other headings, call numbers, authors and titles on the projector plate with his felt-tip pen and ask different children to locate these titles.

Returning to the subject heading HORSES - STORIES, the children are asked if they can locate this heading in the card catalog. This brings up the problem of locating the correct drawer, with which the children may need assistance. In this manner the use of the drawer guides is taught in an incidental manner, but at the time when it is needed, and this proves to be the most successful approach. Other subject headings should now be used, though care should be taken to select subject headings that are of interest to the children for they will use this activity as a selection aid as well as a learning situation.

The rest of the card is now shown to the children by use of transparencies, and the various parts are explained, including any notes that may be imprinted on the card.

A good follow up activity is to give the children ditto copies of a subject card with lines drawn to the various parts of the card. The children are asked to tell what these various parts are by writing the information on the lines. While the children are completing these sheets the librarian and teacher move among the group offering any assistance that might be needed to ensure correct answers. Those schools in which the library program is graded may be tempted to use these sheets for testing purposes. It must be pointed out that this is a learning situation, not a testing time, and it is most important that the children put down the correct answers to help reinforce the learning already accomplished. The process should be a relaxed one, without the pressure of achieving good grades. Where testing is necessary for grades or as a check on the success of reaching objectives, the testing should be done after the entire teaching of the card catalog has been completed, and should be an individualized performance or behaviorial type testing rather than a question-answer written test.

At one time it was suggested that the children be taught to construct a catalog card on the theory that if they could prepare one, they could use one. The attempt to use this method consumed a great deal of teaching time, and produced no better results than the method already described.

The next card used should probably be the title card because it is generally the next in frequency of use by the children. This is followed by the author card, instruction on which should include an introduction to pseudonymous names. The methods for teaching the use of these cards remain the same as those used for the subject card. These cards should consume less of the librarian's teaching time since the uses for most of the information on the cards have already been mastered.

No other cards are taught at Clearlake Oaks because the subject, title and author cards are the only ones used by the children. There seems to be little reason to clutter an already overcrowded catalog with useless entries.

The cross reference cards are simply discussed and some practice given in their use. Further practice comes during the work with index usage where cross references occur with a greater frequency than in the card catalog.

The audio-visual catalog is in book form with listings under titles and subject headings. This index is taught through discussion, practice, and game activities in which material is located through the use of this aid. No special difficulties have occurred with this method of teaching.

The vertical file and individual picture file are housed in subject folders, and are taught by the same methods as the audio-visual catalog. These prove simple for the children to use once they have made the acquaintance of the card catalog.

In libraries where these materials are incorporated into the regular card catalog, they should be handled along with the other cards, requiring only the mention of color bands or other method of coding.

Film strips and educational films may be used in the

teaching of the card catalog, as well as commercially prepared programmed materials. Some of this material is used at Clearlake Oaks for review purposes, not for the initial teaching. There are some differences in cataloging procedures and these can be confusing to children. Once they are able to use the tools with some degree of understanding, these differences can easily be explained, and these commercially produced materials become excellent devices for review.

The Story Hour

Though sometimes it is fun to simply pull up the cushions and relax while listening to a story, more time will be spent at this grade level in selling and sharing of materials. It is a good idea when the opportunity presents itself, to give some attention to the differences between a story and its movie or television version. This activity points out the fact that many stories are adapted to the particular medium, and that it is not always safe to see a movie or TV program and use this as the basis for a book report. Short drama is fun, and often a poem such as Casey Jones can be dramatized on tape with background music and sound effects. There are many classroom art projects that can be built around story characters or incidents. One fourth grade class made their own papier-maché "Dr. Suess"-type characters, and a few of the children attempted rhyming stories about them. Another class took nearly a year to design and construct a large mural of folklore characters using bits of paper, stones, bottle caps, wire and any other colorful materials they could find. They not only developed a mural which still hangs at the school, but all of them could tell you about Paul Bunyan, Pecos Bill and many other folklore characters.

Classroom teachers will occasionally request a story related to social studies, holidays, seasonal or classroom work, and sometimes an unusual event will point up a story that should be used at that time.

Other Activities

The librarian may wish to extend the work with the dictionary, and perhaps introduce some other reference tools, but experience has shown that the children at this grade level are still quite immature, and that postponing the work until the fifth grade offers greater opportunity and need for more comprehensive work in these areas. It is probably best to leave this work to the classroom teacher at this grade level.

One librarian expressed the feeling that the fourth grade outline presented too much material to cover in a year. The library, like any other class, will take the children where they are in their development, and will carry them ahead as far as possible. There is no desperate need to complete all of the suggested work in any one year. It must also be remembered that no suggested course outline, such as presented here, can possibly satisfy all the needs in every library situation. The outline's utility lies in its presentation, as examples, of suggestions and demonstrated sequences and techniques that have proven successful in one more or less typical school library situation. It is doubtful that any library could utilize another library's outline in toto and be completely successful.

Chapter 8

The Program in the Fifth Grade

The library instructional program at the fifth grade level is concerned with the parts of a book, the uses of the table of contents and the index, map work in preparation for detailed study of the atlas, using the encyclopedia, and some work with the opaque projector as a means of reporting. The story hour is continued.

The year's work should begin with a general view of the rules of the library, charging procedures, shelf arrangement and location, call numbers and the use of the card catalog. This review should be accomplished through the use of games, direct questions and answers, filmstrips and educational films when these are available.

A testing technique has not proven successful for review purposes, probably because the review is a re-teaching situation more than a check on what the children have retained from their previous work. It also presents the librarian with an opportunity to offer some instruction for new students coming into the system with limited library backgrounds.

The Book

The children are already familiar with the title page, and many of them will know the location of the various parts of the book. Nevertheless, a period of work on the definition and location of the various parts should be offered. A ditto sheet that has been divided into three columns is given the children. The first column lists the terms: Title Page, Table of Contents, Illustrations, Introduction or Preface, Glossary, Appendix and Index. A second column is provided for the children to write the words front or back depending upon the location of the part, and a third column provides space to write the definition of the term. The ditto sheet and discussion is followed by the game "Stump." A child comes to the front of the group and the others ask him for a definition of a term, its spelling, or its location. The child must demonstrate the part and answer the question. If he is stumped and cannot provide a correct answer, the student who asked the question may take his turn.

The first detailed study is of the Table of Contents. This is accomplished through the use of transparencies, discussion, and ditto practice sheets. It has proven more successful at Clearlake Oaks to begin this work with transparencies rather than with the actual book.

A sample table of contents is made up, usually representative of collected biography, though any typical contents table listing specific subjects would probably work as well. The discussion of the transparency includes such questions as:

> You are asked by your teacher to locate a brief biography of Columbus. Could you find it in this book?
>
> Would you have to read the entire book to find the information that you need?
>
> What pages in this book would you read for your report?

Discussions of this kind could be carried to almost any length, but it is usually sufficient to acquaint the children with the use of the table of contents as a means of locating broad areas of information in the book and to determine if the book may contain a desired piece of information.

The transparency may be followed with a ditto sheet if more work seems to be necessary. The ditto sheet should be the same format as the transparency, and the same general types of questions should be asked of the children.

The children also need a discussion on the use of the chapter titles in a fiction book as an aid to their book selection. It is fun to read the title and contents of a new acquisition with which the children are probably not familiar, and to have them see how closely they can guess the general plot of the story. The librarian should be careful to select a book that is likely to be of interest to the children, because some of them will want to charge it.

Another useful activity is to have the children draw from a hat a slip of paper containing an easily located subject such as "the moon," "George Washington," or "robins," and then locate a title which has this subject listed in its table of contents.

The use of index requires more time to teach than the table of contents, but the techniques used are the same. It should be pointed out to the children that, while the table of contents gives the broad areas of the book's coverage, the index offers a more detailed listing of the contents of the book. This discussion serves to introduce the first transparency used in teaching the use of the index.

The initial index entry introduced to the children is quite simple. The one used at Clearlake Oaks is demonstrated here:

> ROBINS, 22-38; description, 22-23; food, 25, 28-30; migration, 36-38; nests, 24, 26-27.

The discussion begins with a problem. The children are reminded that when they used the table of contents they were looking for a broad area of information, such as all about robins. Now, they do not want to learn all about robins, but only about their nests. "How will you locate this information?" The librarian will almost always get a correct answer, though someone may suggest skimming the chapter to locate the information. Such comments are welcome, for they help reinforce the use of the index as an aid that makes work easier and less time-consuming.

The question, "How many pages are there on nests?", will almost always bring a wrong answer, for children will usually count as they do in arithmetic and miss the first page in a series. They should be allowed to guess, and puzzle over this a bit. If a child comes up with the correct answer and can explain how he arrived at his conclusion, he should be allowed to play teacher for a bit with some of the other entries. Where the answer is not forthcoming, the teacher or librarian should count the pages to show the children how the correct figure is determined. This activity helps point out to the children the correct page on which to begin their reading.

The children need to discover the reasons for the various puncuations, and this can be done by the same question and answer method. Other questions should be asked, such as "Would this book probably contain information on the bone structure of the robin?" Such questions can lead to all sorts of suppositions and conclusions which the librarian may pursue in depth, or not, as he chooses.

This work is followed with a ditto sheet listing two or three index entries, and the children are asked to complete questions similar to those asked when working with the overhead projector. These ditto sheets should be individually corrected by the students as the questions are answered, so that any errors can be corrected as soon as possible.

Reinforcement may be handled through games or activities in which the children actually use the index entries to locate information which they have been given. Those schools required to test for grades will find these activities suited for this purpose since the actual performance of the child is being tested. These activities also help to reveal those children who are in need of special help, and offer the teacher and librarian the opportunity to work individually with these children.

The list of illustrations, glossary and appendix are usually handled with a simple discussion technique. The fact that all books do not have these parts is pointed out to the children, and simple reasons for these omissions should be given.

Film strips and educational films have been used for teaching the use of the parts of the book, but it has been found at Clearlake Oaks that these are better suited for review purposes than for the initial teaching. Several of the teaching outlines reviewed include the material on indexing in special reference tools along with the work with the regular book index. While there may be no serious objection to this practice, it has been found to be more practical to teach the use of these special indexes while working with the particular reference tools.

Additional activities dealing with the parts of a book are listed in the chapter entitled "Supplementary Instructional Program Activities."

The Atlas

While children in the lower grades may have used an atlas, an encyclopedia and some other reference tools, little has been done with these except on an individual basis as the need occurred.

The study of the atlas begins, not with the book but with map work. Since the common road map is used the most, and is the most easily obtainable in quantity, the work begins with this. A portion of a road map of the children's home area is prepared on both a transparency and a ditto sheet. These are the same except that the transparency contains the long and short distance mileages and highway designations. After a general discussion of the area shown on the maps, the long distance mileages are discussed, and the children enter these on their ditto maps. The shorter distances are discussed and these too are entered on the ditto maps by the children. The same is done with the highway designations. Since several roads are drawn on the map the children are now asked to compute the shortest distance between two points on their map. This should be followed by a story. Mr. Jones travels from one point to another, then another, or he may retrace part of his route. The children should compute the distance he traveled.

The children observe as the librarian completes the legend showing the road conditions or types of roads indicated by the various markings. The children are now asked what is the best way to go from one place to another. The map should point out that the shortest way is not always the best way. They should then complete the legend on their own ditto maps.

The children are now divided into groups of two or three and each group is given a road map. Usually, they spread these out on the floor. If the librarian has collected these maps from the same oil company, they will be similar and some confusion can be avoided at this time.

The children are asked to compute the distances by different routes from their community to some other town, road junction or point of interest. They should also note the type of roads, using their legend, and this is a good moment to point out warnings that may be printed on the map such as those for desert roads.

The children are now asked to locate a community with which they are not familiar. Many of them will search all over the map until it is located. If the community is located quickly, another should be given the children. This activity will point up the use of the location charts and guide numbers, and their use should now be taught through discussion and practice with the maps.

Using their legend, the children should now be asked to locate a campground, a recreational area or park near their home town. They should also be given a community to find and asked its population. Other map designations such as railroads, lakes, boundaries and rest areas on major roads should be noted. All of these activities are designed to teach children the use of a road map, but they also develop a working knowledge of guide numbers and the importance of the legend, both of which are necessary in using the maps in the atlas.

How to draw a map is a unit of work included at Clearlake Oaks. However, since this is done to meet a need of the teachers, and not as a necessary adjunct to the teaching of the atlas, this work is outlined in the chapter dealing with the supplementary units.

The next activity takes the children to the atlas where demonstration techniques are used to show the different kinds of maps--political, economic, climatic and others--

and the use of the index as a means of locating the information they need from a map. This work does not take too long because the children have a background of experiences which they are able to apply to this new situation. If the classroom teacher wishes, the librarian may extend this map work to other types of maps such as the contour map or city street maps.

The Encyclopedia

The encyclopedia is not difficult to use. The principle teaching problems lie in the different methods of indexing and in the different spine markings. These are best handled by demonstration-discussion-use methods followed by practice in actually using the easier reading sets to locate material.

The use of the cross references found in indexes is taught here. This is accomplished by discussion, and usually presents no problem because the "see" and "see also" designations are almost self-explanatory.

It must be pointed out to the children that their common supposition that the use of the index is more time-consuming than relying upon the spine markings to locate their information is not always true, and they should be encouraged to use the index. The children also need to be made aware that the encyclopedia gives only a brief overview of most subjects, and that they need to locate other materials for depth study on their subject.

Though the encyclopedia is discussed at Clearlake Oaks as outlined, it has been found more profitable to do any study in depth on an individual basis as there is frequent need for this tool. The method may appear to be somewhat hazardous, but since the eager student will use the tool readily, and the less interested person will use it because he feels it is the easiest way to complete an assignment, the librarian should find ample opportunity to work with most of the children.

Where further work is desired at this grade level, the study booklets available from the various encyclopedia publishing houses are excellent and should be used.

Use of the Opaque Projector

There may be instances where the classroom teacher will not wish to have children use such hardware in reporting, but most teachers will welcome the occasional use of such equipment, and it can be handled very well in the library.

The children are acquainted with the use of the tape recorder, and adding the opaque projector to their list of available reporting techniques is not difficult. Usually the problem is to persuade them to avoid exclusive use of the equipment even when other methods of reporting would be more efficient.

The principle of the projector is explained to the children, and usually the science teacher visits the library period to handle this. Some of the safety precautions are discussed, and the rules governing the use of such audio-visual equipment is explained.

Each of the children has the opportunity to place a book or flat picture in the machine and to focus it on the screen or blank wall. They also run a strip of pictures through the machine, and discover how the roller is used. This is followed by a sharing of opinions on how the projector could be used to aid in the presentation of a report. A volunteer is then found to give his next classroom report in the library rather than in his own room. The librarian helps him prepare his report, and the student presents it to the group. He then acts as a resource person in his own class, assisting others with the preparation of reports presented with the overhead projector.

A follow-up period should be used to explain the situations where this piece of equipment would be helpful, and to give some instances where other means would be best.

The Story Hour

The story hour is continued on much the same format as in the fourth grade. It is desirable to have the music man visit the class to read some of the simpler operas to the class and to play some of the selections from the music scores. This age group will also respond with a great deal of enthusiasm to dramatizing a poem or a section of a favorite story. This has been done at Clearlake Oaks, with the band providing background music, young engineers providing sound effects, and readers handling the parts. These are taped, and classroom teachers frequently charge them out for use in their own classrooms. The favorites have been "Casey Jones," "Homer Price and the Donut Machine" and the cat and the painkiller incident from Tom Sawyer. These tapes have been used for P.T.A. meetings and by the local Women's Club.

The suggested activities for the fifth grade should consume all of the librarian's teaching time. However, the librarian must never develop the attitude that a certain quota of teaching must be completed, with the last lesson and the last period neatly coinciding. The last period of the year will come, but there is really no ending to the activities that can be offered the children in the development of good library habits and attitudes. The year ends, but the following September the librarian simply picks up where he left off and continues. The old adage, "He who moves fastest goes shortest" may never be more true than in working with children in the library.

Chapter 9

The Program in the Sixth Grade

The program in the sixth grade begins with a careful review of the various skills which have been taught in the previous grades. This review is handled through games, discussion, question-answer techniques and demonstrations by the children themselves. Particular attention should be given to the rules of the library and to charging procedures, especially in those schools which terminate their elementary system with this grade. In such systems the children may feel that their seniority gives them privileges that were never intended, and general discipline may be slightly more difficult than in the lower grades.

The work with the sixth grade includes a further extension of the dictionary skills, a deeper study of the atlas, introduction of such reference tools as the almanac and a Who's Who, and an explanation of the Dewey Decimal System.

The Review

The review of rules, charging procedures and use of audio-visual equipment and any special materials owned by the library should be handled by discussion and explanations, paying particularly close attention to the reasons for each of these regulations. These discussions should be carefully planned, and the children given a ditto sheet outlining the material to be covered. This procedure serves to introduce the library to any new students who may be in attendance, and forestalls any "I didn't know" excuses.

The skills review at Clearlake Oaks is handled mostly through game techniques. This method has proven to be the most enjoyable for the children and produces good results. The most successful of such games are outlined in the chapter on supplementary activities.

The Dictionary

The main focus of the librarian in extending dictionary skills is upon use of the unabridged dictionary. Though this has been used earlier by some children, any teaching of its use has been on an individual basis as need arose. The work starts with the special sections found in these dictionaries, and a "search until found" is used for the initial introduction. Usually one of the entries from the signs and symbols section is used and is printed on a large piece of paper. The librarian gives the class a hint by announcing that the meaning for this symbol will be found somewhere in the unabridged dictionary. "Would someone like to see if he can locate this?" The rest of the children go ahead with the browsing portion of their period while the selected student carries out his search. If he cannot locate the symbol, the librarian helps him. Before the children leave the library, the student demonstrates the location of this information in the dictionary. The children then each draw from the "hat" a slip of paper. Each slip has a question that requires the use of the special sections for an answer. The children are asked to come to the library during the week and see if they can locate the answer to their question. The next period is used to discuss the successes and failures of the children. This discussion is followed by a demonstration of the various sections and the information that they contain. Since these vary among dictionaries, the librarian will adjust his discussion to the material available in the edition owned by the school library.

This procedure is usually sufficient to acquaint the children with these special sections. If more work is desirable, the librarian may organize other search games or give the children questions to answer using these sections.

It might appear that simply to give each child a work sheet containing a list of questions to be completed would be a good method of teaching this part of the library work. However, such work proves monotonous to those children who discover the information sources quickly and who do not require as much work. Others will lose interest before they have completed the work sheet and will simply quit. Those children who find it difficult to learn from written work need the visual-hearing-activity technique, and the small percentage who wouldn't complete a work sheet anyway, do get something from the discussions and activity.

Such things as pronunciation, derivations and parts of speech may or may not be covered in the library depending upon the amount of work given the children in the classroom and the desires of the classroom teacher. When it is determined that the library should do this teaching, it is best accomplished by use of transparencies, followed by ditto sheets, using the same techniques as were used in teaching the use of the index and table of contents in the fifth grade.

Some publishers of good dictionaries will provide the library with workbooks, and most of these are excellent, as are the available filmstrips and educational films.

The Atlas

The children are familiar with the road map by the time they reach this grade, and know how to use the location charts and guide numbers. They now need to learn to use the various types of maps in the atlas and to use the charts.

The map work is handled through discussion and activity programs. The various types of maps are demonstrated. A good way of doing this is to remove sample maps from a discarded atlas, mount them on paper and use them with the opaque projector. They are simpler to handle in this form than the actual book itself. The book may be simply held up to show the maps while they are discussed, but if the group is very large, not all of the children will be able to see, interest will soon be lost, and the success of the demonstration will be undermined. The discussions are followed by having the children prepare maps, such as climate, rainfall or economic maps. Whenever possible, the classroom teacher and librarian should coordinate their work so that the same maps will serve a real purpose in the classroom. Such maps as the weather map, geological maps and contour maps may be handled as a special map project correlated with the science program, if the classroom teachers so desire. Otherwise, instruction on these maps, along with discussions on such topics as projections, should probably be left to the classroom, or at least until a higher grade level.

Most children do not find charts difficult to read and, as a rule, require only a little experience before becoming comfortable with them. At Clearlake Oaks, a transparency is reproduced from a distance chart. The children find this interesting and are soon able to carry over the skills they have learned to other charts in an atlas. The children take turns finding the distances from a location near their home to other places in the world. It is fun to have them guess a distance, and then check it. They may also guess whether it is farther to one point or another and then check the distances to see if their guess was correct.

Other charts may be used, and the types of information they contain should be discussed. Once the children discover the value of these charts as sources of information for their research work, they will use them and develop their skills through practice. Individual help should be given by the librarian when the children bring their research problems to the library for solution.

If the library contains special subject atlases, these should also be introduced at this time, and their specialized information discussed.

Specialized Reference Materials

One librarian, who reviewed the manuscript of this book, expressed the fear that many of the children at this grade level would not have developed sufficient reading skills to be effective users of such research tools as the *World Almanac*, *Who's Who*, yearbooks and various handbooks. The introduction of these tools should probably be left to the discretion of the librarian. At Clearlake Oaks there have been classes which could work successfully with these tools and which were ready to use them. There have been other classes for which the introduction of these materials would have been pointless; in these cases work was postponed until a later date.

Such things as a subject index to poetry and a sports encyclopedia need to be introduced to the children. They will find these both interesting and useful. It is usually sufficient to describe the contents of these materials, and to make the children aware that such information is available to them. One good method is to ask the class, for example, for Babe Ruth's lifetime batting average. Then hold up a sports encyclopedia and tell them it will give them that information. Once you show them, locate the answer, and you are into a sports discussion and the use of the sports encyclopedia without pain. The same technique may be used with other special indexes and encyclopedias on special subjects.

The Dewey Decimal System

No attempt is made actually to teach the Dewey Decimal System. This is best left to the professional library school. However, the children should learn a few of the basic number divisions, why they are used and how they are determined.

The work begins with a discussion of home addresses and why we have them. The parallel can then be drawn between their home location and a book location. However, the home address tells little about the occupants of the home, while the call number may tell quite a bit about the book. "What subjects do you think you will find on the 500 shelf?" Two or three children are allowed to go to the shelf and read some of the titles. These are listed on the plate of an overhead projector, and discussion techniques are used to point out that this area contains science and math. "What number would indicate a biography?" Some of the children will already know, but they should be asked to check against the shelf to be certain.

A location game or two should be played requesting the call numbers for a certain topic; or, given a topic, the children can be asked to locate the call number on those books containing information on the subject. The discussions and games will give many of the children a fair knowledge of the meaning of the Dewey numbers at the hundreds level, and this should be sufficient, for the children are likely to have little use for the further subdivisions. Though some librarians may disagree, it has been found that children of this age pay relatively little attention to the call numbers other than to determine whether a book is fiction or nonfiction.

How the Dewey numbers are allocated is demonstrated through a bit of ridiculous play that is fun for the children, yet serves the purpose very well. The children are asked to give the librarian a subject heading. If the subject selected were dogs, the librarian would then write "dogs" on the top of a large sheet of paper on an easel board, the overhead projector, or a blackboard. Now, any number in the hundreds is assigned as a general number for dogs. This number is now written on the paper under dogs. But, the children are told, when they read the book more carefully, they will discover that the book is only about dogs with black coats and that they must assign a decimal number to show this. When the discussion is complete, the chart may look like the following which was developed by one actual class:

Dogs	634
Black dogs	634.2
White dogs	634.3
Fat dogs	634.5
Fat, black dogs	634.25

Such an activity, of course, can be carried on at almost any length, but it should probably be continued only long enough for the children to see that each added number further limits the subjects. If the teacher or librarian wants to carry this a bit further, he may ask the children to select a subject and build their own number system.

The librarian should now show the children the volumes of the Dewey Decimal System, and they should be allowed to observe as a new title is assigned its number. This demonstration is necessary to prevent the assumption by the children that the librarian simply decides arbitrarily upon a number or a system for this one library.

The children should also be told that there are other number systems in use, but that the principle remains the same. Those few elementary schools which use the Library of Congress classification system should use the same teaching techniques, for they will work just as well as with Dewey.

Other Research Materials

The children at this grade level need to be taught how to use the filmstrip projector, and should be encouraged to use filmstrips in their research and reporting. Several hand-held viewers should be available for charging from the library and for home study purposes. The same is true for cassette tapes. The library should have two or three light portable recorders for use by the children, and they must be taught to use them. In order to prevent tapes from being erased the clips on the notched edge of the case should be broken off, or a cheaper model recorder with no recording head should be used. Items such as the du Kane equipment should probably not be charged because of the weight and expense. Nor should educational films, difficult to replace realia, or expensive or delicate models be charged out for home use.

Story Hour

Many of the stories enjoyed by children of this age are much too long to be read during the story portion of the library period. However, an occasional excerpt from a story may be read, or a short story or magazine article used. Considerable attention should be given to new acquisitions of special interest, and it should not be forgotten that children of this age will still enjoy an occasional reading of one of the picture books, a fairy story, or a folk tale. It is fun to take a picture book with no words, and develop a story to fit the pictures. Children often enjoy "modernizing" a fairy story and sharing it with the class.

Poetry should be utilized, but extreme care should be taken in the selection. Boys of this age are all men, and they consider anything like a row of flowers blooming along the banks of the river very much beneath their manhood. Any attempt to force such selections on them, regardless of the merit of the poem, may give them a feeling against poetry that will last a long time. At this age, while the quality of poetry should be considered, it is perhaps not as important as the subject matter. Boys, in particular, are "tough," and they want adventurous subjects. Things like "Casey Jones," "Casey at the Bat," "The Cremation of Sam Magee" and "The Deacon's One-Horse Shay" are among their favorites. The purpose of using poetry at this level should not be to develop a sense of what is fine as opposed to what is not so well written, so much as to develop a feeling of appreciation for this literary form. Girls are not quite so sensitive about the subject matter and since they also enjoy the same type of poetry, it is probably best to give more consideration to what will appeal to the young "men" in the class.

Terminating the Year

Those schools which terminate the elementary system at the end of the sixth grade will probably find it advisable to close with a final quick review of all the work covered. This should be done with games and similar activities which are not arduous for the children. Those systems which continue on through the eighth grade will find other interesting activities in the chapter on supplementary programs.

Chapter 10

The Program in the Seventh and Eighth Grades

The seventh and eighth grades are combined for the purpose of outlining suggested library activities, even though in a school system these grades may be separate, departmentalized or organized on some other plan.

The preparation of suggested teaching outlines is difficult for these years. Considerable differences exist among libraries in the amount and diversity of materials offered in their collections, and among school systems in the emphasis given to particular areas of the curriculum. The interests and capabilities of the students vary greatly, and the librarian must provide materials both for the college bound student and for those who will find their future in the trades and in business. The collection and the teaching materials must also contribute toward maintaining interest in libraries and books, a difficult task at an age when students' interests are expanding rapidly and tend toward more active pursuits. The librarian's problems are often compounded by a lack of sufficient funds to provide the wide range of materials necessary to meet the interests of the students with a wide range of reading levels and to meet the varied academic needs of the school curriculum.

For these reasons this chapter presents a group of topics from which the librarian can choose, rather than a carefully selected and prepared outline of the kind presented for the lower grades. The one exception is the continued work in research and reporting. Though such work is primarily geared to the more capable student, those with limited abilities usually find it interesting if the librarian is careful to keep the requirements within their capabilities. Even children with quite severe learning difficulties will respond when they are allowed to select topics of interest to them and to utilize printed and audio-visual materials with which they are comfortable.

Time must also be found for the sharing of good literature. Short stories, selections from novels, interesting speeches, poetry, essays, editorials, magazines, newspapers, tapes and transcriptions should all be used. Any formalized study of literature should be developed by the language staff with the librarian acting as their resource person, even though the librarian may do much of the actual instruction. Perhaps the main objective for this work at the Junior High level should be the development of an appreciation for good literature; the recognition of those criteria which characterize the better material and, it is hoped, which offer a defense against the ever-increasing amount of trash appearing on book shelves and magazine counters.

The criteria for the selection of personal materials should also be considered. Such discussions should probably include the following:

1. The basic reference materials for personal use at home and school. It should be pointed out that personal needs will differ, and that while materials which will never or seldom be used may look nice on a book shelf, there are less expensive home decorating methods.
2. The determination of what should be purchased and what should be borrowed. The school and public

libraries may be used as a personal collection and, unless the material is going to be used regularly, it is perhaps better to borrow from a library than to purchase.

3. The various bindings and types of printing may be important. When frequent usage is expected, the better bindings may prove to be more economical than less expensive editions.

4. Dealing with book salesmen may present some problems. The actual needs of the material must be considered, and some knowledge of honest marketing practices builds a defense against the few unscrupulous sales people who prey on the unwary. Some mention of the purposes and services of the better book clubs should also be included in any discussion of marketing practices. It is most interesting to include in any discussion of marketing, a visit by one of the salesmen who regularly call on the schools. These people are usually willing to take some time from their busy schedules to do this, and they bring an air of authority into the classroom or library that children are generally willing to accept.

5. Proper care, storage and handling of a home collection, and simple repair and cleaning of materials should be discussed. An interesting discussion sometimes develops when a child has the problem of recovering materials he has loaned. This can lead to an art project in developing personal book plate designs--a project which might also interest the art department.

6. The selection of materials intended as gifts should also be considered, for the frequent question,

"What can I give him?" can often best be solved by a magazine subscription or a well chosen title dealing with a hobby or other special interest.

Research and Reporting

The amount of research the children will do depends to a large extent on the size of the library collection, the teaching practices utilized in the school system, and the capabilities of the students.

The more common tools, such as the atlas and encyclopedia, are being used with a considerable degree of skill by the time the children reach the junior high school grades. They now need to be introduced to the more specialized tools in the library collection, such as the Junior Reader's Guide, the subject indexes and the National Geographic pamphlet file.

It is unnecessary here to discuss each tool individually since their teaching will utilize much the same methods as were used in teaching the use of indexes and the card catalog. Transparencies and discussion, followed by a ditto practice sheet done in class where supervision will keep errors to a minimum, appear to be the most effective method. There are good filmstrips and educational films available on the use of the various tools, and they also should be used. Experience has shown these latter aids to be more effective as supplementary review materials rather than initial teaching media.

The introduction and use of the tools should be followed as soon as possible with practice in their use. The children may select a topic which will satisfy a classroom requirement as well as provide the needed practice demanded by the librarian. This work may be developed into a full report, or may result in a bibliography containing several entries from the tools they are learning to use.

One further problem in teaching reference usage needs attention. Though children are familiar with the use of the tools, and with the contents, they do not always make use of this knowledge when planning their searches. To help them develop a "reference sense" two activities have been used successfully at Clearlake Oaks.

Transparencies are prepared listing different types of questions. These should cover a broad range of available reference materials in the library, but should be designed to illustrate the content material of certain specific tools. The following questions are examples:

> What is the title of the poem who's first line is, "_____________"?
>
> What was Babe Ruth's lifetime batting average?
>
> What was the population of greater New York in 1964?
>
> What is the square root of 96?

The children do not have to answer these questions, only discuss possible sources of information and decide on the best source. Babe Ruth's batting average could probably be located in several sources but a good sports encyclopedia would probably be the easiest and quickest.

The second activity is the reverse of the first one. This is usually played as a game, with a student giving a reference source to another student who then must phrase a question which could best be answered by using the named reference tool. If the latter student fails to phrase a suitable question, the student naming the source goes on to the next person. He wins the game if he is able to go all the way around the room without getting a suitable question.

One more activity should be discussed by the librarian: the length of the report required by the question the student is answering. Several questions, requiring anything from a sentence or two to a full report, are listed on a transparency and the children are asked to comment on the length of the report necessary to handle the question. It is interesting to discuss the method the student may choose for reporting, as well as the length. The discussions can produce some fascinating differences of opinion.

Reporting

The preparation of a formal report is very exacting, and the librarian needs to consider the group of children he is working with when developing this writing skill. The plans for this part of the library program at Clearlake Oaks were developed jointly by the teachers, the high school staff and the librarians. Such planning is necessary to assure adequate preparation of the children for their high school years, and that the high school teachers are aware of what they can expect from their students.

The formal plan for report writing adopted at Clearlake Oaks is a modified form of thesis writing and includes a title page, table of contents, list of illustrations if needed, and introduction, simplified footnotes, and a bibliography.

All of these topics may be taught through a demonstration-practice-discussion technique with frequent reviews and opportunity for individual assistance and questions. This method was used for several years at Clearlake Oaks and at Cuyama, California. The search for a less time consuming and more individualized method led to the development of a partially programmed technique which is included in the appendices of this book. The material has proven successful in two schools in its present form, and at another school where some modifications were necessary. The material is offered here to demonstrate the method of teaching and may be copied by any librarian who wishes to try it.

When possible, several Master's theses should be borrowed for the children as examples of a completely formal report. The various parts should be explained and attention drawn to the care taken to avoid any errors and to the general neatness of the report.

When working with the footnote, two important points should be stressed: the reason for using footnotes, and the information that requires footnoting. The actual form of footnotes does not present many problems to most children, but they sometimes become confused as to what they should footnote. This can generally be avoided by giving the children a specific list of the types of information which should be footnoted. The list used at Clearlake Oaks includes four points:

1. Any direct quotation;
2. Any number such as a population, an area or a date;
3. Any picture or other illustrative material cut from a magazine or discarded book;
4. The meaning of any foreign term, phrase or coined word.

The children should be encouraged to put their material together in a rough pencil copy of the finished report to be submitted to the librarian or teacher for checking. The checking of this pencil copy should be done in an individual conference, preferably in the librarian's office.

The final copy must be in ink, should contain as few errors as possible, and should be enclosed in covers.

It is most important that the children understand that

the librarian is interested in the form and neatness, and that he will check these as well as intelligent use of the reference tools. While gross errors and deliberate sloppiness must be avoided, the librarian does not have the time to proofread each paper for grammatical errors and misspellings, though this may be done by the classroom teacher when the children have selected a topic to meet the demands of a particular class as well as the library.

The children also need a deadline on these reports. While these should be individualized, there are a few children who will never complete their reports unless they have a date when they are due. The children must also understand that they may submit their reports for evaluation at any time prior to the date on which they are due.

Topics for longer formal reports will generally come from one of three sources. The children may elect to do a paper on a topic required by a teacher as a part of their class work; they may select a topic of particular interest to them; or they may ask the librarian to suggest a topic. Since the study of our government is required in California for all eight grade students, many of the topics selected deal with some aspect of civics. However, topics have ranged from the geography and economics of France to surfing.

The remainder of the librarian's class time should be spent in individualized work assigned to reinforce weak points in the children's knowledge or skill in using the library and its materials effectively, or on topics selected from the supplementary list suggested in the final chapter of this book.

General Review

The library work in the elementary school should end with a good general review of library skills. This is done at Clearlake Oaks by using a panel question and answer game. Three boxes of questions are prepared and are ranked according to difficulty, with values of one point, five points and ten points. The librarian selects five panel members to start the game, and each member takes a turn, selecting a question by point value. If a panel member answers correctly, he is awarded his points. Should he fail to answer correctly, he earns no points for that question and must select another student to take his place on the panel. No student is allowed to sit on the panel a second time until all class members have had an opportunity to participate.

The game generally takes three to five weeks to play, since it is only played for the first ten to fifteen minutes of each library class period. The winner is the student with the most points, and a prize is awarded at the annual spring awards assembly.

The high school staff should find their new students quite adept at using the library and its materials, and capable of continuing with higher level work. The high school librarian will appreciate a note listing those incoming students who have given good service as student librarians and who would be interested in continuing with this work in high school. Particular mention should be made of any students who may demonstrate an interest in future professional work in the field of library science or education. While no professional person would want to exert undue pressure on students, their natural interests should be encouraged, and it is a real pleasure to see a young person you have helped train, enter the field of your own interest and choice.

Chapter 11

Supplementary Instructional Program Activities

Beyond the basic areas of instruction there are a number of topics which can be handled through the library instructional program. The few suggested here are only samples of the many possibilities.

Map Drawing and Map Work

Children draw maps for many reasons. Most of them enjoy the artiness of the project, but the activity also assists them in forming a mental picture of the locations and shapes of the countries and places of the world. Specific skills can be developed, including the use of various art media, printing and neatness. Development of confidence in the children's ability to create is a factor to be stressed here.

At least some children have difficulty in developing within themselves the belief that they "can do." To help overcome such fears, the children are told that they need not produce an exact representation of an area; that, since these maps are not going to be used for navigation or survey work, it is not necessary to draw each crook and bend along a border or a coastline. They only need to reproduce the general outline. Tracing, however, is not allowed. There are usually protests in the beginning, but as the children discover that they save time and that their work can still be satisfactory, they come to rely less and less on tracing. Even the unartistic student relaxes in this work when he discovers that his efforts are acceptable.

Once an area is outlined, the printing needs to be done. A simple and satisfactory method is to lay a ruler down on the map and, using it as a guide, print each letter so that the bottom of all letters rest against the ruler. If a little care is taken regarding uniform height of the letters, the resulting work has a very neat appearance. Stencils, of course, may be used, but they are cumbersome and time consuming.

When the printing is completed, the map should be colored. Almost any art medium may be used, but crayon is usually the best. The crayon is held on one end with the side resting on the paper, and is dragged along the margins of the map. The pressure creates a heavier color along the borders, fading toward the center area of the map. The entire map is not colored, but the result gives the impression of being colored, and the method is quick, simple, and very pleasing. The children should also square off the legend area, and use their rulers for the printing.

A demonstration of these techniques is given by mounting a large sheet of drawing paper on the easel board where all can easily observe it. Some mythical island is generally used as a model, and the children suggest town names, rivers and other map entries. When the map is completed it is mounted on the bulletin board, either in the library or the classroom, where it serves both as a model and a reminder while the children do their own practice maps. The same techniques may be used for economic maps, climate maps, or any other type that the children might construct.

The classroom teacher may wish to introduce other

media for map work than flat, drawn presentations. Papier maché, clay, powdered asbestos, plaster or cement may be used to make relief maps, or the area may be cut from colored construction paper and mounted. When several areas are to be shown, the areas may be cut from different colored construction papers and mounted like a jig-saw puzzle, leaving a bit of the mounting surface showing around the edges to serve as a border between the various areas.

A very large map of an area may be drawn in chalk on the black-top of the playground. The children use these maps for relay games or other play activities that help them learn the location and shapes of various places in the world.

If the classroom teacher wishes to move deeper into the study of maps, the library may be used as a meeting place for visiting personnel of the Forest Service, Bureau of Land Management or other conservation agencies who can discuss the use of such items as contour maps, surveys and trail maps. City maps of various types may also be presented by personnel of the City Engineer's Office or the Department of City Planning.

Additional topics might include map projections, sources for maps other than the local filling station, early maps of the world such as Columbus may have used, trip maps such as those produced by the California Automobile Club, and, occasionally, one of the cartoon-type maps sometimes found in travel pamphlets and gift shops.

The topics that can be discussed are only limited by the depth of study desired by the teachers, and the needs and interests of the children.

Writing, Illustrating and Binding an E Book

The purpose of this project is to demonstrate how a

book is put together, and to provide additional work in creative writing and art. The only reason for selecting a topic suitable for the E section of the library is that children often feel these are easier to write, though, in actuality, they are among the most difficult. When a child cannot think of a story, he should be encouraged to do an alphabet book, a book of numbers, or to re-tell a story he already knows.

Ordinary white wrapping paper has been found to be very satisfactory for this work because it is inexpensive and large enought to be cut into quarto sheets. After the initial pencil and scrap paper planning stage, the children complete their finished production on the quarto sheets.

Binding is done with an ordinary needle and thread, and, if the librarian has saved the covers from discarded books, these can be covered and used for the covers of the book. End papers may be plain or decorated, as the student chooses.

When the project is completed the children may either keep the books they have made, or they may be placed on a special shelf in the E section of the library for use by the younger children.

There are several good educational films on the manufacture of a book, and these should be used, along with discussions, in the project. When possible, a visit by an illustrator is most helpful, and a field trip to a book manufacturing plant is highly desirable.

The History of Books, Magazines and Printing

This is another topic of nearly limitless boundaries, and the librarian will have to decide how far to go with it. A number of good publications and educational films are available, and older magazines, newspapers and other materials should be available whenever possible for examination and discussion. Many such examples are available in reprints. An afternoon spent prowling second-hand bookstores is interesting, and may also yield some valuable additions to the historic collection of the library.

Where a museum is available, such as the Huntington Library in the Los Angeles area, a field trip is an absolute must. The librarian should plan to take only a small group at a time. Large groups cannot see, cannot ask, and miss many of the values of such a trip.

Using printed illustrations as models, some children may enjoy reconstructing their own Horn Book, or making a scroll. It is also fun to make a comparison between a reprint of an old Sears Roebuck catalog and a current issue. The author is reminded of a call he received one day from a local druggist who wanted to know what in the world a youngster would want with a "Small bottle of Patterson's Skunk Oil Balm." The youngster had found an advertisement in an old magazine he had charged from the library's historical collection, and wanted to know if the skunk oil was still on the market!

Related Art Projects

There can be little harm in having fun, especially when it accomplishes a purpose, and most children find construction and drawing fun. All sorts of art projects can be developed around literature. The mural depicting folklore characters, which has already been mentioned, is only one example. Below are listed a few other projects that have been used:

1. The construction of costume dolls representing

characters from stories, using a soft drink bottle or plastic container for the body form, and a papier maché head. These are fairly easy to make. The Clearlake Oaks library has a number saved for display purposes, including Snow White, Casey at the Bat, Paul Bunyan and Father Sierra.

2. Papier maché and ceramic characters. These also can be actual historical characters or fictitious --for example out of a Dr. Seuss story. The library also has a few of these including Mr. Toad and the Space Cat.

3. Flat drawings of all types and using any medium available to the children. Sometimes it is fun to place a picture under the opaque projector, trace it, and color it. This is an exceptionally good project for the fearful or the disadvantaged child.

4. Dramatizations of all types. These can be performed on the stage, presented informally in the classroom, or placed on tape with sound effects and background music. The construction of an 8 mm movie is a very good project, requiring all sorts of research and presenting writing and technical problems which the class must solve. This type of project need not be as costly as some people think, and it is well worth considering. These movies have been produced at Clearlake Oaks for as little as eight dollars.

5. Some children might like to write an incident from a story, or adapt a whole story to their street language. Unless the librarian is familiar with their jargon, the finished work may not make much sense, but it does to the children. In one situation, with

which the author is familiar, this technique has been used with considerable success in a Junior High Remedial Reading program.

As an alternative to using the language of the street, a simple modernization of a story may be chosen. Snow White, for example, might leave for the forest to join the Dwarf 7 Combo and end up falling in love with the group's arranger and riding off to a Broadway hit on the back of his Honda one-seventy.

Other Sources of Reference Materials

Today there is a wealth of free or inexpensive materials available to those who know where to look. Travel bureaus of the various states, consulates or information bureaus, government agencies, private companies and even individuals in the community are all sources. The library will find the few dollars spent in subscribing to one of the catalogs of sources for free materials to be a good investment. Care should be taken, however, not to accumulate useless material simply because it is free. The children should be encouraged to preserve their materials, and to donate them to the library's vertical file so that they may be shared. Where material must be returned, as in the case of films, the library should assume the costs of postage and insurance.

All requests for materials should be on school letterhead, and must have the approval of the classroom teacher or the librarian. A convenient method of handling these requests is to have the child make an appointment with the library clerk or the school secretary to dictate his request.

Huck Finn Day

Whatever you call the day, it is one of simple fun, and may occur at any time during the year. The children select a character they would like to represent, and wear an appropriate costume. Sometime during the day, preferably in the morning before hard play tears things up, an assembly and parade is held. At this time prizes are given for those categories which have been selected for judging.

This is a good activity for the Student Council to plan and conduct with the aid of their advisor. Activities such as these, however, should never be forced on any child. Some will not choose to participate for one reason or another and this should be their prerogative.

Book Reviews

Book reviews of new acquisitions or of titles whose circulation may have fallen off may be published in the school newspaper, or may be collected in a folder and placed near the card catalog where they may be helpful to other children in selecting books.

A related activity is to give the children examination copies of titles being considered for purchase, along with a check sheet of the more common selection criteria. This activity may help create an awareness of good literature, and of the physical characteristics of well planned and manufactured materials. This same process may be used with magazines and audio-visual materials, though it should not be more than an occasional activity. Some teachers have found this to be superior to the usual book report, since it offers a real purpose for the reading.

The above are only a few of the many possible library program topics that can be utilized. Each librarian will probably have his own favorites, as will staff members in his school. Situations will demand different treatments, and changing times will bring new and different demands upon the library which will have to be met by different teaching techniques.

It is hoped that this little book, either because it stimulates disagreement or a desire to enlarge upon it, will encourage other librarians to publish their study outlines and share with the rest of us their knowledge and experience so that the instructional programs in school libraries may be improved.

Appendices

The following pages include programmed teaching materials and study-discussion outlines. They are offered as examples of these teaching techniques.

Any librarian or teacher may use this material if he wishes, or may adapt it in any way to his own use.

Appendix A

Programmed Booklet: Call Numbers for Fiction

To the Student:

You have drawn a map of the library showing shelf arrangement of the books and you can walk directly to any given shelf in the library.

You know that the library is arranged in alphabetical-number order from left to right.

Now you are going to learn to use call numbers so that you can find a book in the library quickly and easily.

When you have completed this program you will be able to:

1. Show your teacher or librarian the spine of a book.
2. Show your teacher or librarian the call number on the spine.
3. Tell your teacher or librarian the meaning of the letter J in the first part of the call number.
4. Tell your teacher or librarian where we get the second letter in the call number.
5. Tell your teacher or librarian why we have the second letter in the call number.
6. Tell your teacher or librarian which kind of books have only two letters in the call number.
7. Locate and bring to your teacher or librarian a book when you are given the title and call number. You will be able to do this in one minute.

You will be given a test to show that you have learned the material. The test will cover only those points listed above. There will be no trick questions, and no questions that are not covered in this book.

Each page is divided into three sections. Each section is numbered. Be sure you read the frames in sequence, going from frame 1 to frame 2 to frame 3, etc.

You will read through the entire book once, then turn back to the beginning and read another set of frames through again, and repeat the reading for the third set of frames.

You may work just as fast as you want to, but be sure that you work carefully.

Please read carefully each frame. Some of them will have a blank space in which you will write your answer. Some will ask you to circle an answer or to draw an arrow.

After you have completed your answer, please turn the page. You will find the correct answer in the LEFT HAND MARGIN of the next frame.

If you find you have made a mistake, go back and read the frame over again. Correct your answer, but please do not erase your incorrect answer or scratch it out. Your mistakes are not used to give you a grade. They are used to help make this program a better one for people to use.

Let's try a frame and see how it works.

1	The name of your librarian is ________________ Write your answer on the line. Now turn the page to frame 2 and check your answer.
25	
49	

This type of book is called a PROGRAMMED BOOK. It is a new way of teaching. Some PROGRAMS are written like this book. Some are written in a book form, but you must skip all around in the book to read it. Some PROGRAMS use a machine that you must work.

No matter how the material is presented, it is PROGRAMMED INSTRUCTION, and it is fun, it is different, and you can work at it just as fast as you wish. Please remember though, this only makes it easier for you to learn, it does not "learn" you. You have to put some thought and care into it yourself.

2 Mr. Bowers	The correct answer is here. This is easy and fun to do. Now turn the page and begin.
26	
50	

1

Hey diddle diddle, I've got a riddle:

What part of a book
Rhymes with vine?

You have one too,
It's called the sp _ _ _.

25

We are rested, so let's continue

Dick Smith wrote a book. He is the author of the book.

If you wrote a book, you would be the __________.

49

Brown

B

Bill Smith is the author of a fiction book for the 8th Grade.

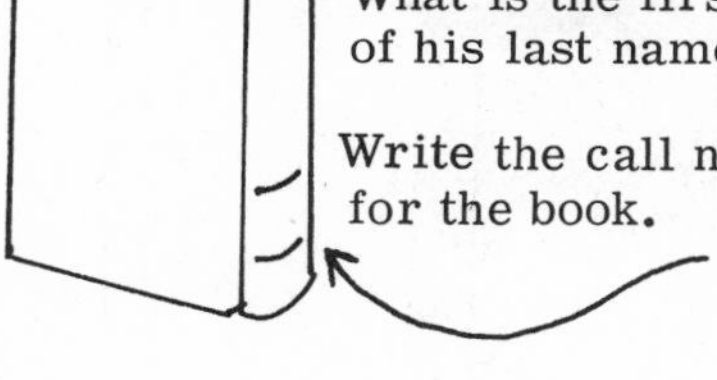

What is his last name? ______________

What is the first letter of his last name? ____

Write the call number for the book.

2

Sp i n e

You have a back bone called your SPINE.

The back of a book is also called the _____.

26

author

The person who writes a book is the __________.

50

Smith

S

Mary Jones is the author of a fiction book for 6th grade people.

What is the author's last name? __________

Write the call number for her book

3

Spine

The arrow points to the book's ________.

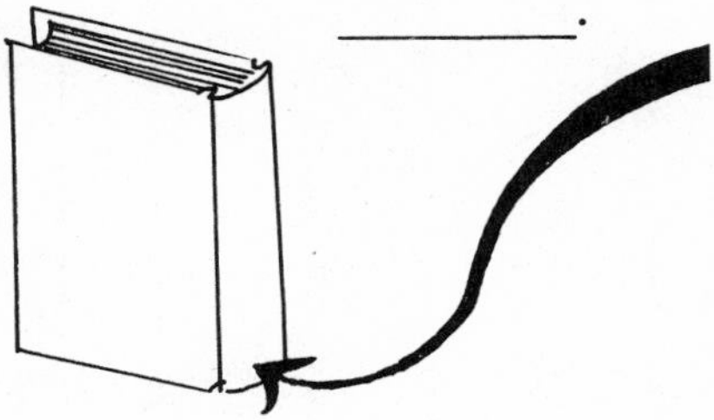

27

author

Let's pretend that you are the author of a book.

When you finish the book, you will sign your name to it.

Write your last name on the line. ________

51

Jones

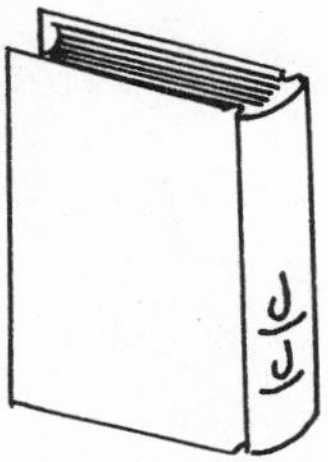

Pete Thomas wrote a book for the 5th grade.

Write the call number for his book.

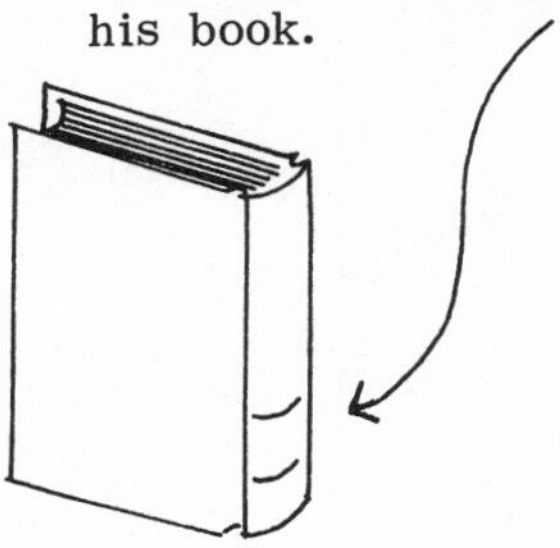

4

Spine

Use your pencil to color the spine of this book.

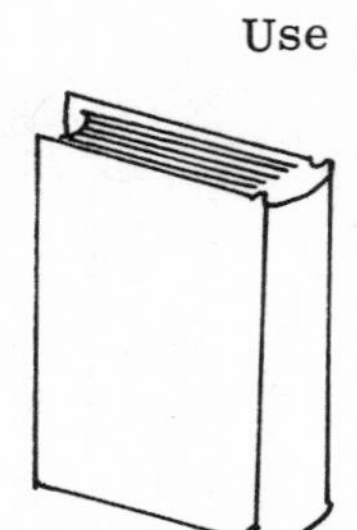

28

Did you write your last name on the line? If I had written the answer to this question, I would have written Bowers because that is my last name.

What is the first letter of your last name? __________

52

The second letter in the call number of a fiction book is the _____ letter of the author's last ___________.

5

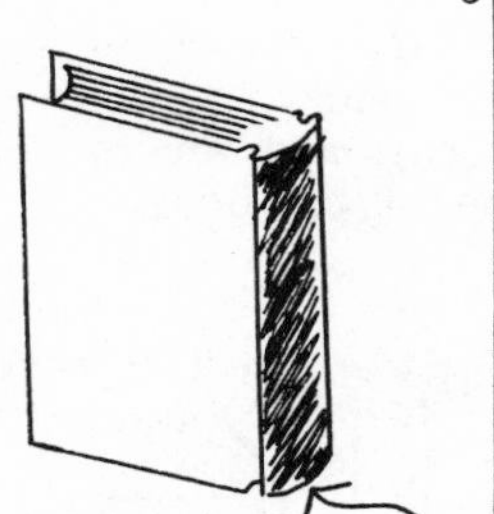

Did you color this part of the book? You should have.

You use the telephone to c_ _ _ a friend.

998-3298 is a telephone n_ _ _ _ _ .

Write these two words again on the lines below.

c_____ n__________

These two words are a part of a book.

29

Did you write the first letter of your last name? Good, you are correct.

Suppose the fiction book you wrote was for children in the 4th through the 8th grades.

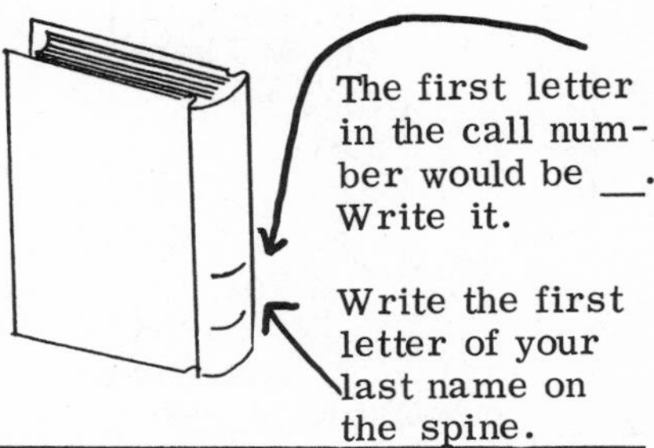

The first letter in the call number would be __. Write it.

Write the first letter of your last name on the spine.

53

1 st.

name

Samuel Clemens wrote the fiction book Tom Sawyer. This is a good story, but it IS NOT A TRUE STORY. It is fiction.

Homer Price is a good story too, but it is not a true story. It is a f______ book.

6

call

number

call number

The call number is a part of the book.
The call number is on the spine of the book.

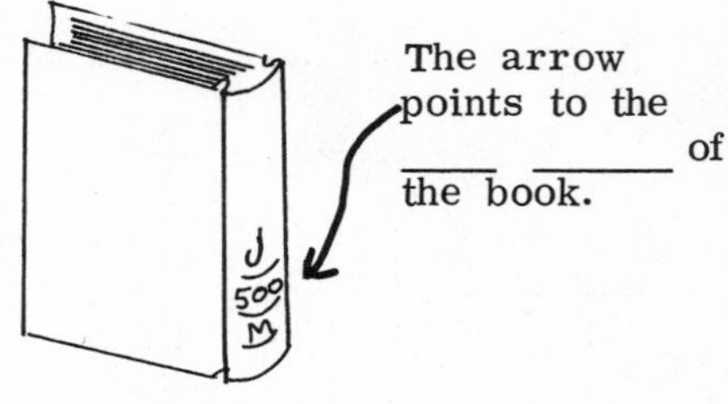

The arrow points to the ____ ______ of the book.

30

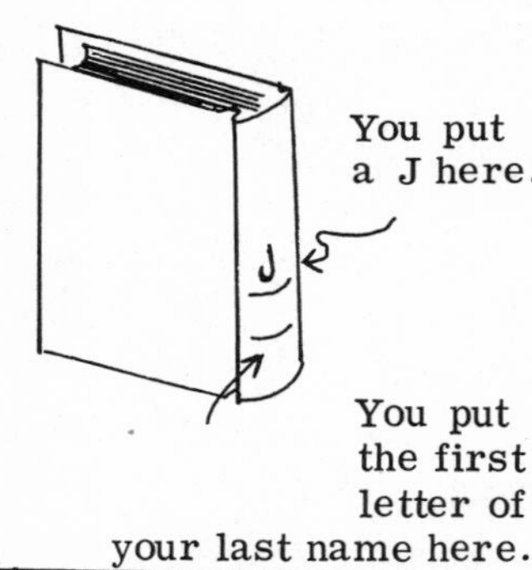
J
You put a J here.
You put the first letter of your last name here.

Dick Smith is the author of a fiction story for the 7th Grade.

What is his last name? ______

54

fiction

Stories that are not true are called fiction.

Tom Sawyer is a _____ book.

Homer Price is a _____ book.

7 call number	J 626 is the ___ ______ P for this book.
31 Smith	What is the first letter of his last name? ________
55 fiction	Samuel Clemens wrote Tom Sawyer. the call number for this book is J C There is no number in the _____ ___________.

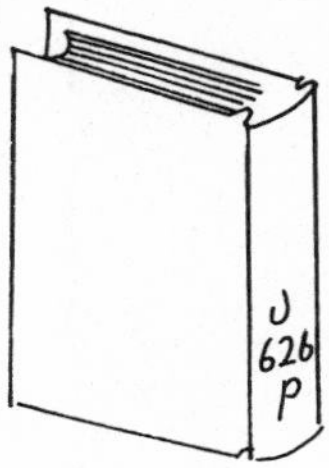

8 call number	The call number on the spine of this book is ____ ____ ____

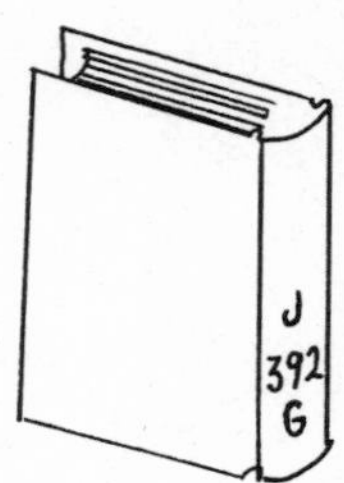

32 S	Dick Smith's book was a fiction story for the 7th grade, so the first letter in the call number will be ____. The first letter of his last name is ____. This letter is the second part of the call number. Write the call number for the book. ____ ____
56 call number	fiction books do not have a number in their __________ ________.

9

J
392
G

The back of the book is called the ________.

33

J

S

J
S

Mary Thomas wrote a fiction book for the 6th grade. The call number for her book will be ____ ____

57

call number

J This call number does not
K have a number, so we know it is the call number of a ________ book.

10

Spine

The letters and numbers printed on the spine of a book are called the ________.

34

J
T

If your teacher wrote a fiction book for the 5th Grade, the call number would be
______
______

58

fiction

Which book is a fiction story, Book 1 or book 2. Circle your answer.

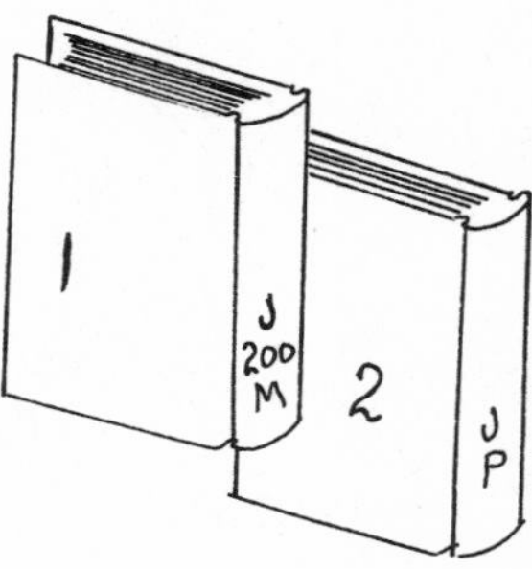

11

call numbers

Put the call number J 500 L on the spine of this book.

35

J
____

____ The first letter of your teacher's last name.

Let's see how well you are doing. Remember, your score is not for giving you a grade. It is used to tell you how well you are doing.

1. The call numbers for fiction books have 1 2 letter in them.
2. The J tells us this is a book for the _____ Grade through the _____ Grade.
3. The second letter in the call number is the _____ letter in the _____________ last name.
4. The back of the book is called its _______.
5. Fiction books do not have a n_ _ _ _ _ in their call numbers.

59

1 (2)

The back of a book is the spine of the book.

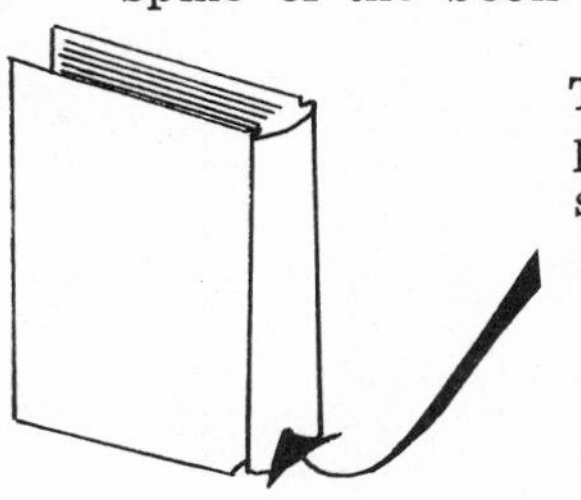

The arrow points to the spine of this book.

12

Both these books have a c___ n_______ on their spines.

BUT: The book on the right (has) (does not have) a (circle answer) number in the call number.

36

1. 1 (2)
2. 4 8
3. 1st author's
4. Spine
5. Number

If you answered the self test questions correctly, please go directly to frame 62.

If you missed number 1, work frames 37-43.

If you missed number 2, work frames 44-48.

If you missed number 3, work frames 49-52.

If you missed number 4, work frames 59-61.

If you missed number 5, work frames 53-58.

When you have finished this work, go on to frame 62 and continue.

60

The back of the book is the

____

13

call number

has does not have

Some books have both letters and numbers in their c____ n__________.

37

All the books in the library have ______________ on their spines.

61

spine

Draw an arrow pointing to the spine of this book.

14

call numbers

Some books have only letters in their _____ ___________.

38

call numbers

Some books have numbers in their _______________.

Other books have only letters in their ____________.

62

We know about call numbers on fiction books. Now we are going to use these call numbers to find books in the library.

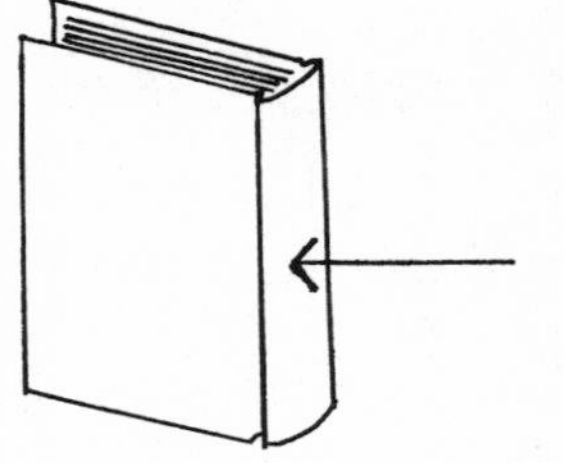

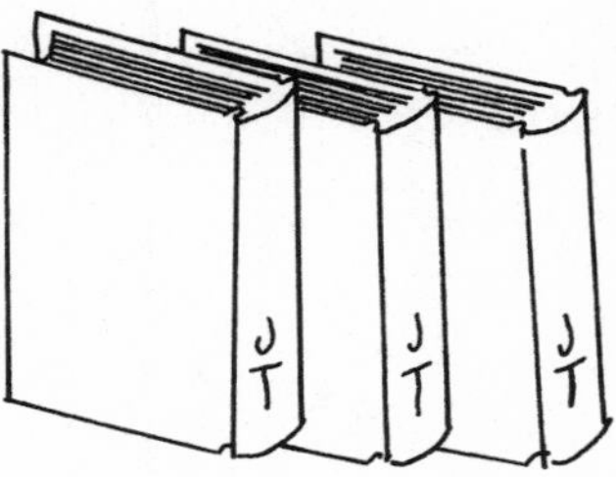

These books all have the same two letters in their ____________.

15

call numbers

These letters and numbers on the spine of a book must have a name, so we call them all ______

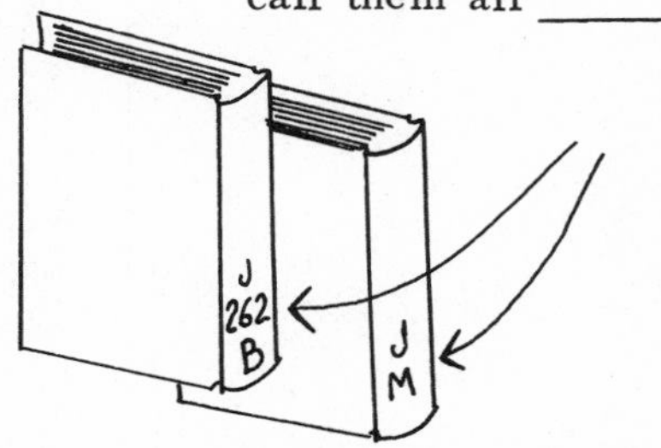

39

call numbers

call numbers

We know this book is a fiction or story book because it does not have a number in its ____________.

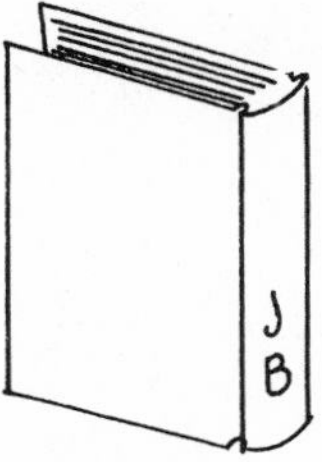

63

call numbers

Books with the same _____ __________ on their spines are shelved together.

All books with the call number $\begin{matrix}J\\M\end{matrix}$ will be shelved t_ _ _ _ _ _ _ _.

All books with the call number $\begin{matrix}J\\T\end{matrix}$ will be shelved __________.

16

call numbers

Call numbers for FICTION or story books do not have a number.

The call number for this fiction book is: ____
____

40

call number

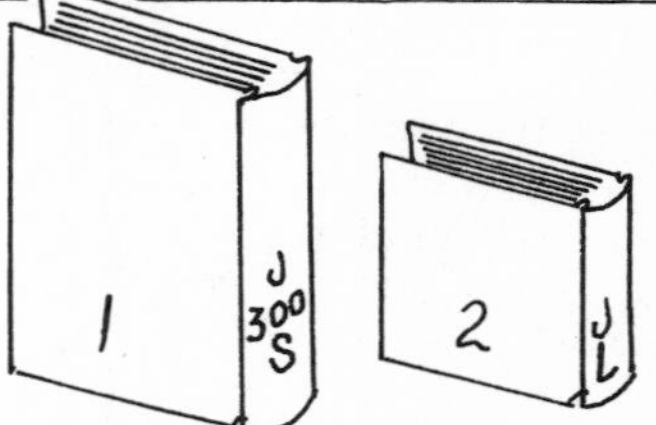

The first book (is) (is not) a fiction book.
circle answer

The second book (is) (is not) a fiction book.
circle answer

64

call number

together

together

One of these books would not be shelved with the others. Which book would this be, 1, 2, 3, or 4? ______

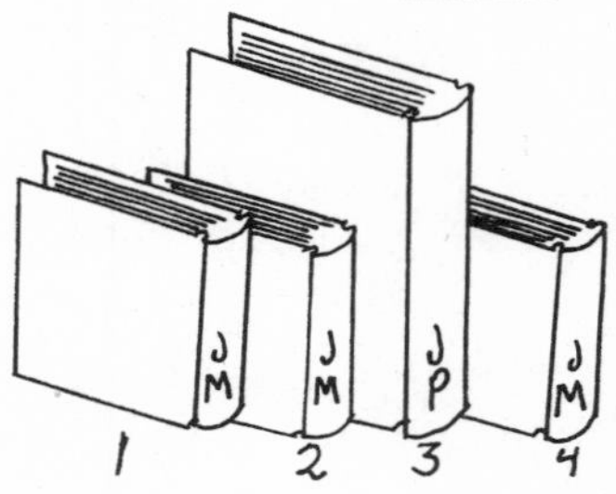

17

J
M

Look at the two books below. We know by looking at the call numbers that the (1st book) (2nd book) is fiction. circle answer

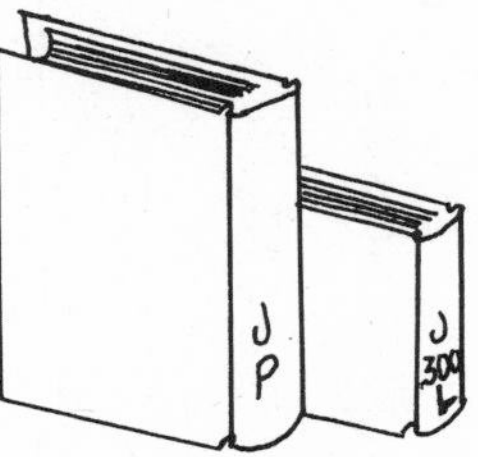

41

is (is not)
(is) is not

We know this is a fiction, or story book because it does not have a __________ in its call number.

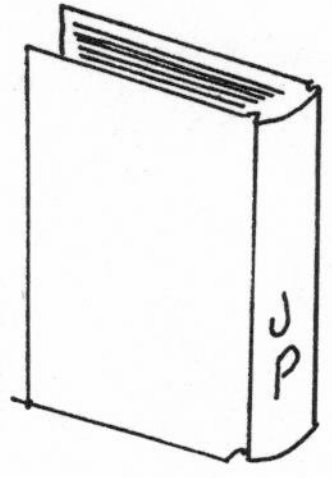

65

3

On the M shelf we will find all the books with the call number J/M

On the K shelf we will find all the books with the call number J/K

On the B shelf, we will find all the books with the call number ____/____

18

1st book (circled) 2nd book

The first letter in the call number of this book is _____.

42

number

See if you can make up a rule now.

A _______________ book does not have a number in its _______________.

66

J
K

J
B

Samuel Clemens wrote the fiction book Tom Sawyer.

The call number for this book would be _____
_____

This book would be found on the ______ shelf.

19 J	The J in the call number tells us the book was written for people in the 4th through the 8th Grades. The J tells us a child in the 1st Grade might find the book (hard) (easy) to read. circle answer The J tells us a person in the 6th grade should be able to read this book. (true) (false) circle answer
13 fiction. (you may have the word story, but fiction is a much better word.) call number	We could say this rule in another way. There are no numbers in the ____ ________ of a ______________ book.
67 J C C shelf	McCloskey wrote the book Homer Price. This book will be found on the _____ shelf in the library.

20

hard easy

true false

If your teacher wrote a fiction book for the 4th Grade, the first letter in the call number would be _______.

44

call number

fiction

This book was written for people in the 4th through the 8th Grades. We know this because the first letter in the call number is ______.

68

J
M

This book would be found on the ______ shelf in the library.

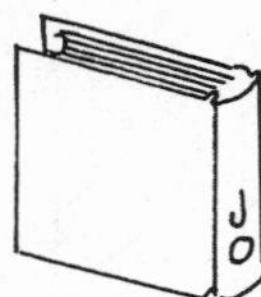

Answer	Frame
21	
J	If your teacher wrote a book for High School students, the call number (would) (would not) circle answer begin with a J.
45	
J	The call numbers for books written for people in the 4th, 5th, 6th, 7th and 8th Grades all begin with the letter____.
69	
O shelf	Go to the shelves and see if you can find one of the mystery books written by Olds. What shelf will you go to? ______ Did you find any books by Olds? __________

22

would (would not)

The J on the spine of a fiction book tells you the book was written for people in the ______ through the ______ Grades.

46

J

This book would be (hard) (easy) circle answer for a second grade student be cause it was written for people in the _____ through the _______ Grades.

70

A fiction book written by Olds would be on the O shelf.

If you want some more practice, try these:

1. One of the books written for girls by Mrs. Wilder.

2. One of Jack London's adventure stories.

3. An animal story by Seton.

23

4th

8th

Circle all the grades for which this book was written.

1 2 3 4 5 6 7 8 9 10

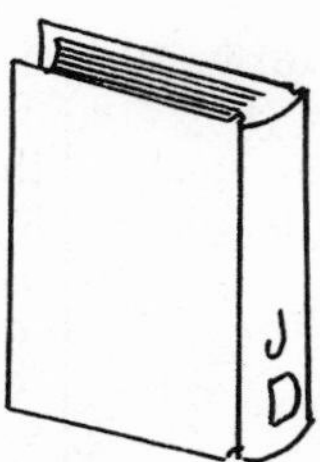

47

hard easy

4 8

A call number for a fiction book has _____ letters.

The first letter in the call number is _____. This letter tells us the book was written for people in the ___ through the ____ Grades.

71

1. The W shelf
2. The L shelf
3. The S shelf

You are now ready for your test to see how well you have reached your objectives. These are listed in the front of this booklet. You may go back over the booklet if you wish.

Please see your teacher or librarian to arrange an appointment for your test.

24

1 2 3 ④⑤⑥⑦⑧ 9 10

Let's rest for a moment before we turn back to the front of the book and start the second set of frames. What have you learned so far?

1. The back of the book is called the spine.
2. Letters, or letters and numbers on the spine of a book are called the call numbers.
3. All fiction, or story books, do not have a number in their call numbers. They only have two letters.
4. The first letter in the call number is J. This J tells us the book was written for people in the 4th through the 8th grade.

48

2

J

4 8

John Brown wrote this fiction book.

J
B

The name Brown begins with a B.

The first letter of his last name is

____

(return to the front of the book)

If you would like to make any comments about this programmed book, please write them here, or discuss them with your teacher or Librarian.

Appendix B

Programmed Booklet: Call Numbers for Nonfiction

You now know these things from your past work:

1. The call numbers are on the spine of a book;
2. J M is a call number for a fiction or story book;
3. The J in the call number indicates the book is for people in the 4th through the 8th Grade;
4. The M, the second letter in the call number, is the first letter of the author's last name. This tells us the title is on the M shelf;
5. You can quickly and easily locate any fiction title when you know its call number;
6. You know that the library is arranged from left to right, starting with the A shelf and going through the alphabet.

Now you are going to learn to use the call numbers for the nonfiction books which all have Dewey Numbers in the call numbers.

When you have completed this booklet you will be able to do these things:

1. When you are shown two books, you will be able to tell which is fiction and which is nonfiction by looking at the call numbers.
2. You will be able to tell your teacher or librarian the names we give the parts of a call number in a nonfiction title.
3. You will be able to tell your teacher or librarian two reasons for using Dewey Numbers in nonfiction call numbers.
4. Your teacher or librarian will give you the title and call number for a nonfiction book. You will be able to locate this book and bring it to him within two minutes.

When you have completed this booklet you will be given a test to determine how well this program has worked for you. The tests will cover only those objectives listed above.

If there are frames which you do not understand, please write the frame numbers down at the end of this booklet, or show them to your teacher or librarian. If you do this, these frames can be re-written so they will be easier for the next students who use this program.

1

"Non" is a prefix that means not.

non-civilized means _ _ _ civilized.
nonhistoric means _ _ _ related to history.
nonhuman means ___ human.
nonfiction means ___ fiction.

16

nonfiction

A horse story has the call number $\frac{J}{J}$.

This is a ____________ book.

30

subject

Books with the same number in their call number are kept together on the shelves.

Books with the call number $\frac{J}{M}$ are kept on the M J L (circle one) shelf.

Nonfiction books with the Dewey number 500 in their call number are kept on the 250 500 M (circle one) shelf.

2 n o t n o t not not	We may say we have two general types of books. These are: 1. Fiction books or story books 2. Non _______ books which are ____ stories.
17 fiction	A book about how to fly an airplane may have the call number J 629.1 M This would be _ _ _ _ _ _ _ _ _ _ book.
31 (M) J L 250 (500) M	Numbers in the call numbers tell us the __________ of the book. Numbers in the call numbers also tell us on which _ _ _ _ _ the book will be found.

3

nonfiction
not

Fiction books are stories or novels. Tom Sawyer is a fiction book.

Books on Science, Biography or Music are not stories. These books are n__________.

18

nonfiction

Science is one of your school subjects. Arithmetic is another of your school s________.

32

subject
s h e l f

Let's review what you have learned.

1. Fiction books do not have a Dewey Number in their Call Number.
2. Nonfiction books do have a Dewey Number in their Call Number.
3. You can tell a fiction from a nonfiction book by looking for the Dewey Number in the Call Number.
4. The Dewey Numbers tell us the subject of the book.
5. The Dewey Numbers also tell us on which shelf the book will be found.

4

n o n f i c t i o n

Homer Price is a story. It is a ______________ book.

A biography of Columbus is true facts. This book is not a story. It is not fiction, it is a ______________ book.

19

s u b j e c t

Social Studies is another of your classes in school. Here you learn about the history of America. Social studies is one of your school _ _ _ _ _ _ _ _.

33

Once, a long time ago, books had no call numbers, and when some-one wanted a certain book they had to search all over to find it. One day a librarian named Mr. Dewey decided it would be much easier if there were some way to find books easily and quickly in all libraries. He spent many years developing the system of numbers and letters that we use today. The system was named after him. His last name was Dewey, so we call the system the D____ Decimal Classi-fication System. The numbers in the call numbers of nonfiction books were also named after him. These are called the _ _ _ _ _ Numbers.

Answer	Frame	Question
fiction nonfiction	5	Churchmouse Stories is a ______ book. The First Book of Stars is a book about astronomy. This book is a ______ book.
S u b j e c t	20	Art is another S _ _ _ _ _ _ you study in school.
Dewey Dewey	34	Fiction books do not have a Dewey Number in their call number. Nonfiction books do have a D______ N______ in their call number.

6

fiction

nonfiction

Swamp Fox is a story. It is a ______________ book.

Your arithmetic text book is a ______________ book.

21

s u b j e c t

You are taking a class in Science in school. Science is the s_ _ _ _ _ _ of the class.

35

Dewey Number

Nonfiction books do have a Dewey Number in their call number. Fiction books do not.

Nonfiction books have a _____ __________ in their call number.

Fiction books do do not have (circle one) a Dewey Number in their call number.

7

fiction

nonfiction

The call number of Homer Price is J M. This is a story. It is a ________ book.

The call number for The First Book of Stars is J 520 P.

This is a ____________ book.

22

Subject

A book on how to make dolls is a nonfiction book. Doll making is the __________ of the book, because the book is about how to make dolls.

If you have a book about science, then science is the ____________ of that book.

36

Dewey Number

do (do not)

520 is the D________ N__________ for stars.

8

fiction

nonfiction

Fiction books do not have a Dewey Number in their call number.

J
M
a

would be the call number for ________ book since there is no Dewey Number in the call number.

J
300
P

would be the call number for a ________ book because there is a Dewey Number in the call number.

23

subject

subject

Nonfiction books are about something. What the book is about is the ________ of the book.

First Book of Electricity is about electricity. Electricity is the ________ of the book.

37

Dewey Number

398 is the ________ ________ for fairy stories.

9

fiction

nonfiction

J
590
L

Draw a circle around the part of the call number that tells us the book is nonfiction.

24

subject

subject

How to train your puppy is a book about training dogs.

Training dogs is the ________ of the book.

38

Dewey Number

You will remember:

J the reading level of the book (4th through 8th Grade)

M the first letter of the author's last name.

What are the meanings for the parts of this call number?

J ________________

590 ________________

P ________________

10

J
590
L

J
P This is the call number for a ____________ book.

J
92 This is the call number for a ____________ book.
B

25

subject

"Story of Columbus" is a biography about Columbus. The book is about the life of Columbus. The life of Columbus is the _________ of the book.

39

reading level

Dewey Number

1st letter of the author's last name

You remember that Fiction books are arranged on the shelf in alphabetical order. They begin on the left and continue right on through the alphabet.

After the fiction books come the nonfiction books. These also are arranged from let to right. The first books will be in the 000 hundreds and continue through the 900's. In our library the 92 books are shelved after the 900's.

Walk along the nonfiction shelves and notice that they are all in order by number as well as by the first letter of the author's last name.

DON'T JUST LOOK AT THE NUMBERS
SEE THEM
READ THEM

11

fiction

nonfiction

Books that do not have a Dewey Number in their call number are __________ books, or story books.

Books that do have a Dewey Number in their call numbers are not story books. They are ____________________ books.

26

subject

A book with the Dewey Number 520 in its call number is about stars.

Stars is the s _ _ _ _ _ _ of the book.

40

Did you really look at the numbers? Did you notice the order?

See if you can locate these books on the shelves.

Book of Holidays

Wonders of the Heavens

Buzztail

Fun with Wire

Young Brahms

12

fiction

nonfiction

You can tell a fiction or a nonfiction book by looking at the call number.

If there is a Dewey Number in the call number, you know the book is a ________ book.

If there is no Dewey Number in the call number, you know the book is a ________ book.

27

subject

A book about airplanes might have the Dewey Number 629.1 in its call number. Books with 629.1 in their call numbers will be about airplanes. Airplanes is the s________ of these books.

41

If you feel you need more practice, your teacher or the librarian will give you some to practice with.

Self test. You will not be graded on this test.

1. A call number with a Dewey Number is a __________ book.
2. A call number without a Dewey number is a ___________ book.
3. Story books are f________ books.
4. Your Science Text is a ________ book.
5. J
T is the call number for a ________ book.
6. J
300
L is the call number for a ________ book.
7. The Dewey Number gives us the s__________ of the book.

13

nonfiction

fiction

Time for a self test. Remember, you will not be graded in any way on this test. If you miss any, you should go back over the frames. Answer T for true and F for false.

1. Fiction books are story books__.
2. Fairy stories, science, music are all nonfiction books._____.
3. J 920 M is a nonfiction call number. _____.
4. J M is a fiction call number.__.
5. You can tell a book is nonfiction when it has a Dewey Number in the call number. _______
6. You can tell a book is fiction when it does not have a Dewey Number in the call number. _____

28

subject

The Dewey Numbers in the call number tell you what the book is about. The numbers tell you the s_ _ _ _ _ _ _ of the book.

42

1. nonfiction
2. fiction
3. fiction
4. nonfiction
5. fiction book
6. nonfiction book
7. subject

Look back at the objectives for this booklet. If you feel you can do what the objectives ask of you, please see your teacher or librarian for your test.

You may go back over the booklet again if you wish.

14

All of your answers should have been marked true.

If you answered any of them false, go back and read frames one to twelve again.

If you wanted to read a story about dogs, you would want to read a fiction nonfiction book? (circle one)

29

subject

J
520
T

is the call number. This call number tells you what the book is about. The Dewey Number, 520, tells you the ________ of the book.

If you have any comments you want to make about this program, or if there were frames you did not understand, please write them in the space below and on the next page. Your comments will help make this a better program.

15

fiction (circled) nonfiction

If you wanted a book on how to train your dog, you would be looking for information, and not a story book. You would be looking for a n___-f__________ book.

(turn back to the front of the booklet to find frame 16.)

subject

(frame 30 is at the front of the booklet.)

Appendix C

Booklet on Footnotes

(8th Grade)

Appendix C

Booklet on Footnotes (8th Grade)

Objectives of this booklet: When completed you will be able to:

1. Write at least three types of information that you must footnote.
2. When given the necessary information you will be able correctly to write a footnote from a reference book with an author, and from one without an author.
3. When given a book you will be able to locate a page which has a footnote and point out to your teacher or librarian the author, title, publisher, date and the pages referred to in the reference.

Please Note:

Do not loose this booklet. You will be expected to have it with you each library period until you are finished, and you must return the booklet to the library.

This booklet is programmed. You will not read it as you do a regular book. You will read and complete frame one. Then turn the page to find frame two, and the answer for frame one which will be on the left hand side of the page. Work completely through the booklet and then turn back to the front to find your next frame. Continue until all frames have been done.

Since you will not be graded on the booklet, there is no reason to look ahead for answers and then simply write them in without reading the frames. The purpose of the booklet is to help you learn. You must help yourself to learn by doing each frame in sequence. If you make a mistake, go back and read the frame again and make your correction.

You will have three weeks to reach the objectives, but you may work as rapidly as you wish. When you feel you have reached the objectives, see your teacher or librarian and they will check you. The questions will cover only those objectives listed above.

Answer	Frame	
Your answers will always be in this block to the left of the next frame. The answer for frame 1 will be to the left of frame 2 on the next page.	1	An author writes a book. The person who writes a book is called the ______________ of the book.
title	7	Frank Hill gave his book the title About Dogs. Frank Hill was the ____________ of the book, and the title was ______ ______________.
	14	The publisher will copyright the book. This is the year that it was published. John May Co. published the book in 1964, and this date becomes the fourth part of the footnote. The copyright date for this book was ___________.
John Giles. A Day In Greece. Day Co., 1960. p. 106.	21	Write a footnote for this reference: Author: John Miles Title: Good Manners Publisher: Day Co., 1966 Pages referred to: 109 and 110.
3 26.	28	Write a footnote for this reference. World Encyclopedia, published in 1960 by World Co. You refer to information in Volume 17 on page 144.

Frame	Answer	Question
2	author	The first thing you have to have in order to produce a book is the _ _ _ _ _ _ who writes it.
8	author About Dogs (be sure your title is underlined)	Write the name of the author (Frank Hill) and the title of his book, (About Dogs) on the lines below. ____________. ____________ (Be sure to underline the title.)
15	1964	Let's write the footnote with these four parts. Author: Frank Hill Title: About Dogs Publisher: John May Co. Date: 1964 ____________. ____________. __________ __________, _______.
22	John Miles. Good Manners. Day Co., 1966. p. 109-110.	This footnote is all mixed up. Write it over again correctly. Over the Hill by Howard Crosby. 1966, Macy Co., p. 13.
29	World Encyclopedia. World Co., 1960. V. 17, 144.	Write a footnote for any page of the Cosmopolitan World Atlas. You will find it on the reference shelves.

author	You will notice as you go through this booklet that each part of the footnote is taken in order of its importance to the book-- the author, title, publisher, date and pages you used for your reference. This is easy to remember.
9 Frank Hill About Dogs.	You have just written the first and second part of a footnote. These two parts were the _____ who wrote the book and the __________ of the book.
16 Frank Hill About Dogs. May Co., 1964. (Did you underline the title and use commas and periods?)	You used a quotation from page 27 of this book. The page on which you took your information is the last part of the footnote and is written p. 27. Write the footnote again using the last part, the page reference. 1 ____________. ___________. _____________, ______. ______.
23 Howard Crosby. Over the Hill. Macy Co., 1966. p. 13.	Author: Rene Jones Title: Dead Cats Publisher: Goul Inc. Date: 1200 Pages read: 15 and 16 Write a footnote to this reference.
30 Cosmopolitan World Atlas. Rand McNally & Co., 1966. p. ___.	Write a footnote from any volume and page from one of the encyclopedia sets in the library. Show this to your teacher or librarian for checking.

3

You have written a book. You are the author of the book. Write your name on the line below. Write your first name first.

____

---

author title

10

Now that Frank Hill has written his book, he wants to publish it, so he sends it to a PUBLISHER. The company that publishes a book is called the P_ _ _ _ _ _ _.

The answer is in frame 17.

17

[1]Frank Hill. <u>About Dogs</u>. John May Co., 1964. p. 27.

The little [1] in front of the footnote is the number of the footnote. This is the first footnote on the page, so it is number [1]. If you had another footnote on this same page, this would be [2]. Notice the number is raised.

Rene Jones. <u>Dead Cats</u>. Goul Inc., 1200. p. 15-16.

24

Some books do not always have an author that you can locate. Encyclopedias and Atlases are often such books. In writing a footnote for one of these references, do you think you would-

1. Leave the author's name out.
2. Make up a name for the author.
3. Use the publisher for the author.
   (select one for your answer)

Title. Publisher, date. Volume Number, page.

31

Find a footnote in one of the reference books and see if you can read the title, author, publisher, date and page numbers. You may use a thesis on the display counter.

4

If your name was Frank Hill you would have written

Frank Hill

Did you write your name like this?

You have just written the first part of a footnote.

11

publisher

The first important thing to a book is the __________ who writes the book. The second important thing is the __________ of the book. The third important thing is the __________ who publishes it.

18

What would you do if the information you used was on two pages? No problem, simply put a dash between the first page used and the last. p. 18-20. You use a quotation from pages 27 and 28. You would write this p.___-___. You use pages 44 and 45. You would write this p.____ ____. You use information from pages 18, 19 and 20. You would write this _______________.

25

1. is correct
2. sorry, you cannot do this.
3. May not be wrong, but we are not going to use this type of form.

When you can not find the name of the author, write your footnote exactly the same way but you begin with the title. You have one less thing to write.

Show your footnote to your teacher or librarian and explain the parts to them.

You should be ready for a check on how well you have reached your objectives. You may look back over the frames again if you wish. When you are ready, please see your teacher or librarian for an appointment.

Answer	Frame	
	5	Can you guess what the second important part of the footnote is going to be? ____________________________
author title publisher	12	Now we can add the third part of our footnote. Author: Frank Hill Title: About Dogs Publisher: John May Co. Write this much of the footnote below. __________. __________. ________. ________, (did you underline the title?)
p. 27-28 p. 44-45. p. 18-20.	19	On the next four frames are self tests for you to judge your own work. If you do the first two without error, you may skip the last two. If you make mistakes on the first two, look back over the frames and then take the last two.
	26	You use information from page 38 of World Atlas, published by Atlas Co. in 1959. Write a footnote for this reference.

If you care to make any comments on this booklet, please write them here and on the next page. Your comments will help to improve this booklet for the next class.

6

Read frame 6 and see if you are correct.

Would you turn in a report or story without a title? Of course not. An author would not turn in his book without a title, so the second important part of the book is its t_ _ _ _.

13

Frank Hill.
About Dogs.
John May Co.

There are only two more things to put down and the footnote is complete. The first is the date of publication, and the second is the page or pages where you found your information.

20

Remember, you ARE NOT GRADED on the tests in this booklet. They only show you how well you have reached your objectives.

Write a footnote from this information. A book written by John Giles and published by Day Co. in 1960 was called, A Day in Greece. You used a population figure from page 106, and this footnote is the first one on this page of your report.

27

World Atlas.
Atlas Co., 1959.
p. 38.

An encyclopedia is the same except that you have the volume number to put in before the page number. Your footnote would read:
Title. Publisher, date. V.3, p.26.

The information tells you you found the information in volume__ and on page____.

Appendix D

Report Writing (8th Grade)

You know now to write a footnote from any book that has an author, and from any book that either does not have an author or for which you cannot find the name of the author.

When you finish this work, you will be able to:

1. Write a footnote from a magazine when your teacher or librarian gives you the necessary information. You will be given a magazine and a page and you will be able to write the footnote for it.

2. Write a footnote from a newspaper that your teacher or librarian gives you.

3. Write a footnote of explanation for a coined word or phrase, a foreign term, or an unusual word that may require definition.

This booklet is not programmed. The teacher or librarian will show you some transparencies which will be discussed. Then he will give you the necessary information, and you will write it down on your paper as indicated.

Please be sure you work correctly, and please, ask any questions you wish at any time during the discussions or work.

Your teacher or librarian will go over this as many times as you may wish but you may ask for a check on your objectives at any time you are ready.

A footnote from a magazine

You will need this information and in this order:

1. The title of the article, and this will be in quotation marks.
2. The title of the magazine, and this will be underlined.
3. The publisher.
4. The date, including the month of publication when this is given.
5. The page or pages you used for information.

You will notice that no mention is made of an author. Often, an author of an article is not mentioned. However, when it is, then his name should be the first part of the footnote.

Below are the two examples used on the transparency.

"How to Grow Roses." Today's Gardener. Harmony House, March, 1962. p. 39.

James Howe. "Care of Small Tools." Home Care Magazine. Peters and Son Co., April, 1960. p. 43-44.

Your teacher or librarian will hold up a magazine for you to see. He will give you all the necessary information. Write your footnote in the space below.

"________________________." ________________

__________________. ____________________,

__________, ______. __________________.

Try another one now, but without so many hints as to how to do it. Your teacher or librarian will give you the information.

Now, take any magazine from the rack and write your own footnote from this. When you are finished, show it to your teacher or librarian.

Footnotes from a newspaper

These are written just like the magazine footnotes except that you will have a date which includes the day, month and year.

Below is the example used in the transparency during the discussion.

> "New Wraps for Bananas." Lake Daily Mirror. Mirror Publishers, March 17, 1969. p. 4.

Your teacher or librarian will show you a newspaper article and give you all the information you need. Please write your footnote below.

"________________________________." ________

______________________. ________________, ______

________, _______. ____________.

Your teacher or librarian will show you one more and give you the information you need. Write the correct footnote reference in the space below.

Go to the magazine rack and select any newspaper to use to write your own footnote. Show it to your teacher or librarian when it is completed.

If you need some individualized help, or want some more practice before seeing how well you have reached your objective, please see your teacher or librarian. If you do not wish to do this, perhaps one of your friends can help you.

Remember, footnotes of explanation are just short statements to explain something you have said or used in your report that may not be clear to the reader. These are easy to write.

You have seen the transparencies and taken part in the discussion, so let's play a bit now.

You have used the foreign word Plitzerquitzel in your report. Please write a footnote of explanation in the space below. (Of course you will have to make up something about the word. Since it is not a real word, anything you make up will be all right. It is only the form you use that will be checked.)

You may try some more if you wish. Your teacher or librarian will check them for you.

Appendix E

Forms for Report Writing

The following pages show you how to prepare your Title Page, your Table of Contents, List of Illustrations, Maps, etc. (if you use any), and your Bibliography. Keep this booklet handy while you are doing your report.

Your teacher or librarian will show you some transparencies and there will be some discussions on these parts. You may take any notes you wish in this booklet.

THE JUSTICE DEPARTMENT

A Report
Presented to
Mrs. Kidd

For
Social Studies

---

by
Joe Larson

April, 1966

THE TITLE PAGE FOR YOUR REPORT

The first thing on the page is the title. This is centered and in capital letters.

The next item is what the thing is (a report) and who it was done for.

The next item is why it was done. In this case it was done for a Social Studies Class.

The next item is the author's name, and the last, the date.

Please notice that the printing is centered on the page. The lines between the various parts of the title page are not necessary. You may use them if you wish.

On the back of this sheet make up your own title page. If you already know the topic you are going to write about, make up the title page for your report. If you have not decided yet, then make one up. Be sure to use the whole page. When you are finished have your teacher or librarian check your work.

CONTENTS

Following the Title Page is the Contents or Table of Contents. You may use either term you wish.

Please notice that the headings are all capital letters, and that the material is centered on the page.

The page number for each chapter is the page on which each one begins. Since each page in the entire report is numbered, even though you may not put a number on it, Chapter 1 will never start with page one.

The last entry on this page is the BIBLIOGRAPHY. This word is placed so that it begins under the chapter numbers. This is because the Bibliography is not considered as another chapter.

If you have already planned your report, use the back of this page to make a pencil copy of your Table of Contents and have it checked by your teacher or librarian. If you have not yet decided, please make up a Table of Contents anyway and have it checked.

Most formal reports also require a list of illustrations, but for our work we are not going to include this. If you particularly want to put this in, your teacher or librarian will show you how to do this. The same is true of an Introduction or Preface.

The last part of your report is your BIBLIOGRAPHY. This is a list of all the materials you used while finding information for your report.

You list everything here, even materials that you may not have used, or that duplicated other materials that you read.

The form is the same as that used for your footnotes except that you put the author's last name first, and you do not have to put down the pages you used. The Bibliography is also in alphabetical order.

Footnote:

1 Frank Hill. About Dogs. John May Co., 1966. p. 45.

Bibliography:

Hill, Frank. About Dogs. John May Co., 1966.

Here are some more examples.

"Man with a Horn." Life. Time Inc., June 7, 1966. p.23.

"Man with a Horn." Life. Time Inc., June 7, 1966.

2 Howard Felt. 101 Ways to Earn Money. Opportunity Press Inc., 1959. p. 18.

Felt, Howard. 101 Ways to Earn Money. Opportunity Press Inc., 1959.

John Goode. Plays for Children. Child's Press Inc., 1959. p.44.

Goode, John. Plays for Children. Child's Press Inc., 1959.

Try writing the bibliography for two or three of the references you have been using. Give them to your teacher or librarian to have them checked.

Index